With hindsight, it might seem that Pam was always destined to follow in her father's footsteps into the world of music. But an unexpected tragedy would almost handicap young Pam to the extent that her dream would be dashed before it was started. The fact that she survived with her life seemed like a miracle to most people. Yet how would she bounce back? Mel had triumped over setbacks and after decades of cruel rejection would soon ride atop country music. Soon Pam would find out if she had her father's resolve and drive to go with the talent and creativity. She was impatient to make her mark, but it wasn't her time just yet. She still had some growing up to do.

Pam Tillis

Out of Her Father's Shadow

ACE COLLINS

St. Martin's Paperbacks

PAM TILLIS

Front and back cover photographs courtesy Everett Collection.

ISBN: 0-312-96404-8

Printed in the United States of America

St. Martin's Paperbacks edition/ December 1997

10 9 8 7 6 5 4 3 2 1

To Branson, Missouri,
a place that has given
many of country music's forgotten legends
a place to work their magic.

Chapter One

In November of 1995, Robert K. Oermann, author of *Finding Her Voice: The Saga of Women in Country Music,* told *USA Today* that women were getting back some of the ground they've lost to the "stampede of hot hunks. The artistic future of country music is in the hands of women because the men right now are such cookie-cutter suburban Merle Haggard wanna-bes."

The widely respected Oermann was probably right. Female singers were finally beginning to package and sell more than just a small percentage of country music's main product—recorded music. In the nineties, women were also making their mark in every other facet of what was once a male-driven industry. Many of country music's top public relations experts, booking agents, and managers, as well as even some of the side players and sessions regulars, were now women. High heels and skirts were replacing boots and wranglers in the offices of CEOs, and in studios from Music Row to Ashland City, the "weaker" sex was on a roll and taking charge in areas that had once been the exclusive territory of a small, tightly knit "men's club."

Yet even while this revolution had been set in rapid-fire motion by big stars like Dolly Parton and Reba McEntire, the public was probably largely unaware of what was going on behind the scenes. Sure, they now heard almost as many female disc jockeys as males, and many of those who had become the most visible hosts on The Nashville Network and other country music television outlets were women, but most folks who bought tickets to concerts or CD's or tapes at one of the nation's thousands of Wal-Marts (country music's top product sales outlets) didn't know who booked the shows, devised the marketing strategies, or played the instruments and turned the knobs in the recording studio. They didn't know or care who hired and fired everyone from the artists down to the janitors, or signed the checks either. All the fans really knew and cared about was who sang the songs.

So where country music fans first noted the emergence of the industry's more feminine side was not in the midst of the larger revolution that was transpiring behind the scenes, but the more noticeable one that had created an environment where the airwaves were now echoing with the sounds of female vocalists almost as often as they did with the wailings of men. Yes, for even the most casual listener it was now rapidly becoming apparent—even obvious to the hard-headed, conservative, gun-toting, beer-drinking, pick-up-driving, drugstore-cowboy rednecks—that no longer was it just the men who closed shows, had the big hit singles and earned platinum records; this money-making world was now open to women too. And the top awards were no longer reserved for men either. It may have taken shape a lot later than it had in Hollywood or New York, but in Music City, times were a-changing, and K. T. Oslin's *80's Ladies* had grown beyond being just the "girl singers" and into some of the business's most influential power brokers.

In the midst of this subtle revolution, Pam Tillis has quietly emerged from a large pack of Reba wanna-bes with more power and control over her own career than any other woman in country music, with the possible exception of the Oklahoma redhead herself. No matter who grabbed such a high level of career mastery would have been a major country music story. Yet because of the things Pam overcame and the odds she faced just to be accepted in country music, her rise to the top in both sales and power represents something far more. The real story of why and how a sweet, somewhat shy and seemingly undemanding second-generation country music songstress quietly and smoothly seized control in areas that were once reserved only for men was anything but a well-scripted plan. As a matter of fact, the groundwork that propelled Pam into doing what had once been considered impossible was laid before her birth. And the man who created the foundation on which Pam would eventually build had even more trouble getting to the top and gaining recognition than his daughter. And that is saying something! So while we are now finally admitting that country music's women have long been handicapped by their gender and this has kept many talents from growing to their full potential, Mel Tillis's handicap may have been even harder to overcome. The odds against his becoming a superstar may have been even greater than those of his daughter becoming her own producer at a major country music record label. Face it, without Mel there could have been no Pam.

A large number of country's newest fans only know the legendary Mel Tillis as Pam's father rather than as one of music's greatest entertainers and songwriters. He was born in the midst of the Great Depression on a hot Florida day in 1932. The son of a baker, Lonnie Melvin Tillis from almost day one was constantly on the go. The Tillises would move more than two dozen times during the first few years of the young boy's life, and this constant picking up and moving on must have put a little bit of gypsy in Mel's soul. He would never fully settle down until five decades later when he built a home and theater in Branson, Missouri.

The most remarkable thing about Mel the child was not that he was athletic, bright, or talented, all of which he was. The most remarkable thing was that all of his strengths were usually overlooked. The fact was that few people saw what should have been his obvious talents because in their eyes he was "cursed." Mel stuttered badly, and back then, a boy who stuttered was the object of ridicule and the blunt end of scores of cruel jokes. Folks with Mel's handicap were often considered "half-wits" or freaks, and even a loving mother couldn't completely hide the slings and arrows that were tossed Mel's way. Before he hit school, most believed that if he didn't outgrow his speech impediment, he would never amount to much of anything. In the midst of a world that was ready to deal out only negativism, it seemed that the only solid strokes the boy received were when a first grade teacher discovered that he could carry a tune. And when he sang, he didn't exhibit a speech problem. The positive reinforcement he received from singing to the children at school and at school programs increased Mel's affection for music. But the metamorphosis really began when he made a trip to visit a friend's church.

Mel fell head over heels in love with music when he heard folks singing Stamps-Baxter, sharp-noted hymnal gospel standards accompanied by flat-topped guitars and cherished hand-me-down fiddles in a Pentecostal revival meeting. It was a sound driven by a spirit that the young boy couldn't shake. That music, as well as the riffs and the runs, tumbled in his head again and again. Then, when he hit his teens, the family radio had added Bob Wills and the Opry stars to that early gospel influence and created a sound that was uniquely his own. While other kids his age were digging Bing Crosby and Frank Sinatra and dancing to big bands, the tongue-tied Tillis was again setting himself apart in an offbeat way by embracing a music most called hillbilly and considered anything but cool. This was the music of ignorant country peasants, but Mel didn't care much about labels or the thoughts of his peers, and by the time he was in high school, Mel was proudly playing the music he had heard on WSM's "Grand Ole Opry" on a cheap guitar he had purchased from his brother. At the time, few realized what that small investment in the old Sears Silvertone acoustic guitar would come to mean in time and money.

Because of his speech problems, Mel was never as confident as most boys his age. Even when he became a high school football star and was winning over folks at local talent shows, he still held back a bit. He lacked self-assurance. Yet that all began to change when he was offered a chance to sing a Hank Williams song on a local radio show. Mel's version of "Why Don't You Love Me Like You Used to Do" made the seventeen-year-old seem like a real star to the boys in his National Guard Unit and spurred the young man on to consider a career in the music business. Yet it would take some time to gain the confidence and experience to carry through on these plans. Later, Mel would be able to offer his daughter a way to show off her musical skills, but if he was going to make the contacts he needed, he was going to have to do it on his own.

Without music, Mel Tillis probably would have ended up working a factory or farm job or spent a lifetime in the military. His stuttering surely would have gotten in the way of his chances to advance in any employment where he would have had to deal with the public on a constant basis. The fact was that even after years of therapy, he had real problems finishing sentences without dragging them out to interminable lengths. But he didn't have to speak at all when he played his guitar and he did have a winning smile. And because a song has a constant beat, he had no problems when he sang either. In the boy's mind, it seemed perfectly logical that music was by far the best road out of a situation that seemed to doom all of Mel's other paths to opportunity even before he took his first step.

After a stint in the Air Force and a dozen different odd jobs, Mel decided to commit himself fully to following his dream. In the mid-fifties, he hitched a ride to Nashville.

Rejected, pushed away, told to pack it up, the stubborn Tillis stayed and began to write songs.

In all honesty, Tillis should have listened to what was happening in Music City and headed straight back to the strawberry fields of home. Elvis and his rockin' imitators had knocked mainstream country music off the charts. Rather than looking for the next Webb Pierce or Hank Thompson, most A&R men in Music City were beating the backwoods for someone who sounded black, spoke southern, and looked like Tab Hunter. Mel wasn't even a close fit on two of these three requirements, and he rarely could sustain a sentence long enough to reveal his own deep southern accent. Nevertheless, he refused to give up. Turned down by the likes of RCA and Tree Publishing, he finally landed a job at Cedarwood Publishing. There he began to crank out some solid original numbers, cut a few demos, and landed a gig as the lead singer for Bob Wills and His Texas Playboys. Ray Price, then the keeper of the shuffle-beat, honky-tonk sound that was fighting rockabilly for chart dominance, cut a few of Mel's original compositions, as did Webb Pierce. Mel even gained a sympathetic ear and cut a few demos for Columbia. Then, just when things were looking up, the world came crashing down.

A Florida girlfriend called and told Tillis that she was pregnant and that he was the father. This news couldn't have come at a worse time. Mel didn't need the added pressure of supporting a family on a meager salary that barely fed himself. He was somehow hoping that this was all a mistake. Yet here was a problem he had to face and he knew deep inside that there was only one right thing to do. Mel's God-fearing, church-going mother advised him to take off and leave the teenage Doris Yvonne at home. She didn't want her son forced into a marriage he wasn't ready for. Yet for one of the few times in his life, Tillis didn't follow or agree with his mother's advice. He married the teenager and the two of them moved back to Nashville where Mel eventually landed a pretty fair job playing rhythm guitar for Minnie Pearl.

Minnie, whose warm style and devotion to her fans, would make a profound effect on Tillis the entertainer, would in the future also impact the life of Mel's oldest offspring. But at this moment, the generous and sweet comedy genius who was paying Mel to play guitar and just be silly Melvin was actually getting in the way of the new husband bonding with his ever-so-young bride.

Mel and Doris's marriage, which began on shaky ground and without the benefit of tried and tested love, was never stable. From the first, the couple would disagree and fight often. The young girl, so far from her Plant City, Florida home, was not equipped to handle the long weeks she spent alone. Nor did she appreciate having to share lodging with other people as the Tillises often did. She wanted her new husband to settle down, move back to their home state, and get a "real" job. Doris needed things. Mostly, though, Doris needed Mel and he was never there. Feeling trapped by circumstances, yet knowing that music was his only chance to really use his talent, Mel struck out at Doris with solid reasons why they were going to have to sacrifice now in order to have a chance at something special later. Yet chasing rainbows didn't appeal to the pregnant girl. Deep down she didn't share, nor did she have faith in, Mel's dreams. Her vision was of a house with porch and man who came home from work every day at the same time. Meanwhile, Mel's sights were on long ribbons of highway leading to smoky bar rooms or dusty county fairs. Frustrated, Doris returned to Plant City, and lived with her mother as the time for delivery drew near. At least there she knew she wouldn't be left by herself for days on end. At least there she had friends and family she could depend on for support and understanding.

For Mel, life now that Doris had left Nashville was much the same as it had been before he got married. He toured with Minnie Pearl, wrote songs at Cedarwood, went out with the guys, and cut a few demo records. Yet in late July, 1957, something happened that woke up the "married but acting single" young man in a big way. Riding through the Kentucky hills with Minnie's band, Tillis tuned in Bill Morgan's radio show on WMAK, a Bowling Green country music station. As he listened to Morgan, a music business acquaintance, spin the latest wax, he received some expected news in a very unexpected way. In a story that has been told many times and was one of the most heartfelt images revealed in Mel's own autobiography, *Stutterin' Boy,* Mel first learned the news that he was a father over the airwaves and piped through a car's radio speaker. It seemed that early during his shift on the twenty-fourth, Bill Morgan had received a call from one of Tillis's musical friends in Nashville. That person had gotten the news from Mel's family in Plant City. As the band sped along the road and Mel casually watched the trees race by in a green and brown blur, the radio blared out, "If Mel Tillis is listening, he has a new six-pound, eight-ounce boy."

Mel was so overcome with excitement that he stopped at the next pay phone to call home. His own father confirmed everything that the new dad had heard over WMAK except that Mel didn't have a baby son, he had a daughter. Hundreds of miles from where she was sleeping in a hospital, Mel saluted his firstborn, Pamela Yvonne Tillis (Doris had named her without much influence or help from the singer/songwriter). The musician had long heard it said that Plant City had the sweetest and biggest strawberries in the United States. The small community even called itself "The Strawberry Capitol of the World." But at this point, Tillis was sure that his new daughter was sweeter than any of the area's berries. And when he finally finished his tour and made it home to see his little girl, Mel informed everyone that Pam was the prettiest thing that had ever made its way into the world. Yet new fatherhood and a beautiful daughter didn't hold him down for long. As soon as Minnie packed her bags to entertain the live crowds, Tillis was back on the road again. While Doris was changing diapers, filling bottles, and adapting to all the changes that came with motherhood, Mel was racing around from date to date and experiencing hardly any change at all.

If Mel had begun life as a gypsy, constantly moving as his father searched for work, then Pam too was going to start life on the move. When the first Tillis child was still in diapers, Mel and Doris moved from Nashville to Florida and back again and again. Every time a door seemed to open wide enough for Mel to get another chance at something more than just musician's wages, he would dash in, usually finding little more than broken promises on the other side. Try as he did, he just couldn't seem to make it big enough to do much more than buy a few weeks of security at a time, and that was hardly enough for a new father and his family. Tillis could sense that it wasn't nearly enough for Doris either. Still optimistic in the face of rejection, Mel pushed on, never giving up, never allowing himself to stop believing in his dream.

Three decades after the frequent mad dashes between the Sunshine State and Music City, Pam herself would tell *People* that some of her earliest memories involved moving. "We packed our '57 Chevy, and a frying pan, an unemployment check, and an old guitar, and we came up here [Nashville]. We had to keep moving back, though. It wasn't as easy as he hoped."

In some ways this constant starting and restarting, as well as her father's struggle to sell himself and his kind of music to a largely uninterested Nashville, would offer Pam a host of practical lessons that would serve her well when she would pursue her own quest in the music business. But in her youth, shifting from Tennessee to Florida and then back to Tennessee, the long hours spent on the road and the rejections and false hopes did little for the family's stability. As a matter of fact, the lack of money and security, coupled with Mel's long hours spent on the road or at the studio writing songs, was driving a deep wedge between him and Doris. It seemed that everyone who knew the couple thought that they were headed to divorce court. If Doris had not become pregnant with a second child, the marriage probably would have broken up.

The birth of another girl, Connie, saved the union for the time being, but it didn't offer much peace. This was still a marriage filled with misunderstanding and heartache. It had more downs and sad times than a Hank Williams song. Yet in spite of failing in his bid to get much support at home, Mel's career was beginning to look genuinely promising. More and more artists were recording his compositions, and he was beginning to make some waves as a singer in his own right. Then all heck broke loose.

Mel and his manager got into a dispute over song profits and royalties. They couldn't settle the matter between themselves in a timely manner, so a long legal battle followed. Tillis's career was put on hold. Months dragged by and with all of his earnings from music tied up by the courts, Mel had no way to provide for his growing family. Sadly, he packed his bags and he, his wife, and his kids left Nashville and headed back home to Pahokee, Florida.

As he set up his new home, an old enemy came back to haunt the struggling father and husband. Mel Tillis's speech problems might have been no real detriment in plying his trade as a songwriter, but it was a different story in the real world. Yet he still had his clever wit and eager personality, he was an engaging, good-looking man, and when he wanted to, he had a suitcase full of charm. Yet more often than not, this was overlooked as soon as he opened his mouth and began to stutter. Just like it always had, as he searched for a solid job outside the music business, the stammering made a bad impression before Mel's personality had a chance to shine through and take over. Because of this, many doors were rudely shut in his face. First he was closed out of the business he loved by a judge just when it appeared that he was really ready to take off, and now he was pushed aside because of other people's false judgments; it seemed no one was willing to give Mel a fair shake.

Tillis finally convinced the owner of Harry's Cookies to give him a shot. It seemed Mel's fortunes had changed when the snack company agreed to try the unemployed songwriter as a salesman. They gave him a uniform, a truckload of cookies, and a brand new route. His job was to take Harry's into virgin territory. In other words, Tillis had to sell this product to store owners and managers who had never before placed it on their shelves. As Mel would soon discover, for a man who had problems expressing himself, this was going to be a herculean challenge.

"I worked for three weeks and didn't sell one cookie," Mel remembered. Mainly he just drove from town to town, store to store, and after he failed to make a sale, tried to keep himself from getting discouraged by singing in his truck. In the face of all of his problems, staying positive was almost as tough as selling the cookies.

"I kept telling myself, 'mind over matter,' " Tillis recalled. "Soon those words turned over in my head and became heart over mind."

With a new song title rebounding in his head, the cookie hawker drove toward his next stop, using his few spare moments to himself to slip into his old vocation. Soon he was cruising through Miami humming an original shuffle-beat four-by-four dance melody.

"Heart over mind, worried all the time," were the first words Tillis fitted into the new tune. The remainder of the lyrics quickly followed. Over the next few days Mel continued to compose in his truck. As the missed sales added up, so did the finished songs. By the end of three weeks he had added "One More Time" and "No Love Have I." With those three tunes in hand, he turned in his uniform and keys and headed back to Music City.

For Doris, who had so hoped that the family could settle down and have a normal life, this return to Music City had to have been a nightmare. It had to have seemed like just another false start, just another move that would tear her away from her family. Yet no matter how hard she tried, by now she also knew that she couldn't keep Mel from dreaming, she couldn't stop him from chasing rainbows. So once again she grudgingly joined him in the Chevy and headed back to Tennessee. Only this time some of her worst fears were put to rest as the results of Mel's rainbow chasing were much more profitable.

Mel was quickly able to sell "One More Time" to Ray Price. It would hit number two on the charts in 1960. "No Love Have I" also found a home with Webb Pierce. It would also jump into the top five that year, and many years later be recorded by Gail Davies and Holly Dunn for hits. In 1961, Price finally recorded the first of the cookie truck trilogy, "Heart Over Mind." Though not as big as "One More Time," this swing tune did make it to number five on the charts. This run of hits established "Mel the Songwriter" as a Nashville staple. He was a dependable tunesmith who could churn out hits. Now, with money in the bank and a heart full of confidence, Tillis could really hit the ground running.

Psychologists have long known that no one can really measure the effect that a parent's profession has on children. The experts agree that this impact has to do with the child's interest, talents, and the way the child views the parent's occupation. It would seem only logical to assume that many offspring will attempt to follow in their parent's footsteps. Many great basketball players are the sons or daughters of coaches. Consider the actors and actresses who grew up watching one or both of their parents in the business. Did these individuals make it in their parents' professions because of inherited talent or just the extra hours spent in the gym or around the studio? Is it genetic or environmental?

Certainly Mel Tillis was a talented musician. He could sing, he could write, he could play, and with his wit, he could also entertain. Pam and her siblings had to have inherited some of this as a part of the natural selection process. Yet the fact that Pam also spent hours listening to her father sing, wandered the country from time to time on a bus, and even fell asleep in guitar cases during recording sessions made music an important part of her environment, too. As she grew from toddler to preschool age, the shy, bashful, and slightly built young girl who rarely spoke to strangers about most things in her life, didn't hesitate when asked what she wanted to be when she grew up. She proudly told those who asked that she was going to be a singer. By the time she was in first grade, she would give almost anyone who would listen her own version of a Judy Garland classic she had memorized from watching the showtune singer on television. Her looks quickly revealed that she was Mel's daughter. Her singing gave strong hints that there was music in her soul.

Yet even with Mel's career beginning to take off for real—by the time Pam entered first grade her father was scoring some modest hits for Decca and later Kapp records—things were not all that great at home. Mel was on the road as many as 300 days a year. When he was in Nashville, he spent much of his time writing songs or in the studio. Left alone with the children, Doris was lonely and often overlooked. And having an absentee father who didn't seem to have much time for those he said he loved had to hurt more than just Doris. Without really knowing it at the time, Pam was suffering in the same manner as many other entertainers' children. Her dad was rarely there to read her stories, sing her a lullaby, play with her in the yard, or go for a walk. It would be understandable if young Pam rebelled against her father by hating the business that was taking him away from her so much. Yet while her mother may have felt bitter about the stolen hours from time to time, Pam didn't really seem to mind. It was, after all, all she had ever known.

On the occasions when Doris would get out of the house

and go on the road with Mel, Pam and her siblings had a baby-sitter by the name of Grace Topply (Rainwater). Grace was a family friend who just happened to be rock-and-roll child-sensation Brenda Lee's mother. Brenda had shaken the world before she herself was a teenager with hits like "Sweet Nothin's," "As Usual," "I'm Sorry," and even a Mel Tillis original, "Emotions." Grace had been there every step of the way to make sure that the small singer with the big voice had a normal life. Yet even though Brenda had spent a good part of her youth doing the usual teenage things, she was still on the road a great deal, too. So Grace knew firsthand the sacrifice in time and energy it took to make it in this business. And because she realized just how lonely being left behind could be, she was the perfect person to come into the Tillis children's lives. With a big hug or a funny story, she could make the lonely days seem bright and sunny. And while Grace loved all of Doris and Mel's kids almost as much as she loved her own, she was especially fond of the oldest.

"Pam was curious, sweet, funny, clever, cute, and very polite," Grace recalled. "Even at a very young age she was a very giving person. Very down to earth. She was not at all impressed that her father was an entertainer. Yet she did love to sing and she loved music."

It was Pam's own love of music that caused her to constantly ask for chances to learn more about it. And these were requests that Mel wasn't going to refuse. At about the time her father was landing a long-term deal with Kapp records, the eight-year-old was taking her first piano lessons. So while Mel was singing things like "Wine" and touring with Webb Pierce, his daughter was playing classical riffs and listening to Wagner.

Even thought he wasn't home much, Tillis still liked to show his kids off. He proudly introduced them to anyone who came by the house on those days when he was there. He also marched them on stage during concerts when they happened to be in attendance to watch his show. He even had them learn a few songs so that they could perform with him from time to time. When Pam was just eight, Mel dressed Pam and her sister up in gingham and had them debut, singing "Hang Down Your Head Tom Dooley," at the Opry. While she may have loved music, her Opry debut, along with the other times her father pulled her on stage during her youth, were not moments that Pam would paste into the "favorite memories" page of a scrapbook.

Pam later told reporters, "I hated it. It was an ego bruiser. I just couldn't stand getting up there and having all that in me (other kinds of music she liked) and having to go through his material. And I felt I was, like, on display; 'Here, he's got offspring.' "

Singing songs she didn't like while wearing outfits she despised on stage may have been one of the major negatives of being the daughter of a solid country music songwriter and a now rising entertainer, but there were some solid benefits too. And a lot of these Pam didn't resent. One was moving to a country home with nineteen rooms. Now with acres to call her own, Pam could spend her hours of spare time wandering around Mel's new farm, exploring, playing, and fishing—a passion that still consumes her few free moments. In many ways Pam was living a "Lassie"-type adventure each day, and it was a great way to grow up. What kept her story from being the "ideal" family television show script was that there was not a happy couple living on the farm guiding her every move. The fact was that her father had a great deal to offer in the way of interesting experiences and famous friends, but very little time to share much about either of those things with his family. He was just working way too hard chasing his vision of the American dream to be a real dad.

With the roving Mel out securing his place in the hearts of country music fans, it should come as no surprise that his daughter first heard "Lovesick Blues" sung not by Hank Williams or Mel Tillis, but by blues vocalist Etta James. And while gospel music framed a great deal of what she loved when she first began playing piano, country music took a back seat to almost every other form of musical expression. In her young mind, country dress, talk, and music were not cool.

Maybe it was because she rarely had time to spend with him, but as Pam grew, Mel's influence seemed to take a back seat to that of the radio and her friends. The fact was that the stuff her dad was bringing home, the things by old-timers like Bob Wills and Red Foley, as well as the hot country acts of the day like Buck Owens, didn't move Pam. Country audiences may have been flipping out to Loretta Lynn, Jack Greene, and Sonny James, but young Pam was beginning to get into Carole King and the Rolling Stones. When she first heard the Beatles, she flipped. Now these folks were putting out real music. Look at the way the crowd was responding to them!

"I never divided music into categories," Pam would recall as she looked back on her formative years. "It was all the same thing to me and I loved it. And even though I was shy, I knew I was going to be a singer someday."

While no one doubted that the young girl loved music, few could picture her on stage by herself. She just didn't seem assertive or confident enough. As her baby-sitter had noted, she was shy and bashful. More often than not she didn't like to call attention to herself. She was much more intent on helping others. Yet unknown to even most family friends, she was expressive and she did dream of taking a mike in her hands, dressing in some mod outfit, and knocking them dead on Ed Sullivan. She wanted to have her own band, tour the world, and see her name in lights. And in her own quiet way, she set about making her dreams come true.

She began writing songs on the piano at the age of eleven. She would come to refer to this as the creative spark "during my introspective early years." Like her father, she was at first turned on to sacred music as a form of expression. Initially she wrote gospel, but gradually she turned to rock and blues to find herself. In 1969, at the age of twelve, she bought her first guitar, and by observing rock and country pickers on television learned how to play. At about that same time, she joined the junior high band and picked up the clarinet.

By the time she hit her teens, that fever had started in full, that passion for music which had so consumed her father had now been realized in the daughter. Just as Mel had gotten into Hank Williams and Bob Wills, Pam would soon be cutting her teeth on Janis Joplin, Bonnie Raitt, and the Allman Brothers. The young lady whom her dad called "Olive Oyl" because of her long skinny legs and big feet was soon completely obsessed by music. In many ways, it was her life. Yet she wasn't ready to share it with the world just yet.

With hindsight, it might seem that Pam was always destined to follow in her father's footsteps into the world of music. But an unexpected tragedy would almost handicap young Pam to the extent that her dream would be dashed before it was started. The fact that she survived with her life seemed like a miracle to most people. Yet how would she bounce back? Mel had triumphed over his setbacks and after decades of cruel rejection rode on top of country music. Soon Pam would find out if she had her father's resolve and drive to go with the talent and creativity. She was impatient to make her mark, but it wasn't her time just yet. She still had some growing up to do.

Chapter Two

In 1991, when Pam completed the liner notes for her Arista album *Put Yourself in My Place,* she wrote that she wanted to thank "My dad for not spoiling me—My mom for being there." To a large degree that was how she spent the formative years of her life. Just like so many children of the fifties and sixties, Pam was caught in a family where the father was completely dedicated to his job. More often than not, the only person she consistently had to turn to was her mother. And it would have been a little hard to spoil his daughter when Mel was always on the road, but it would have also been hard to have blamed him for chasing his dreams when they were so close to being in reach!

Almost everyone who has ever been maliciously ridiculed is constantly seeking acceptance in one form or another. If they feel that they are not considered worthy of others' esteem, they work harder to get it. For Mel Tillis, music had long been his way to overcome all the insecurities brought on by his speech impediment. He also was one of the rare individuals who have such a stubborn will and an intense drive that he gained that acceptance and respect by courageously displaying his own weakness. When people fully saw his weaknesses, they finally noted his strengths too. Yet Mel had even taken it a step further.

He had used his stuttering as a part of his act. Not only did people notice him because of it, it had set him apart, brought him laughs, and gave him a unique identity. Any child could be proud of a father who had overcome so much, especially one who had been so honest and up-front with others about his own problems. While Mel's openness had helped him to build a career, it also had kept him on the road and away from home. So while he wasn't hiding his own insecurities from his fans or the critics, he was, by the very nature of his business, keeping much of what made him special from his family.

Mel was justifiably proud that he was now considered one of the hardest working entertainers in the business. He almost seemed to live to work and he thrived in the glow of the spotlight. As he slowly grew into a star, he was one of the few performers who didn't seem to resent the time his fans took away from his personal life. After all, this was the lesson that he had been taught when he had worked with Minnie Pearl. She had always said, "If you love the fans, they will love you right back." How could Mel not love them? They accepted him as he was, didn't ask him to be anything else, and paid his bills.

So Mel was following the tried and true country music method of crawling to the top. This was the way it had always been done. You knocked on doors, begged people to listen to you, worked long hours for low pay, made your contacts, got a record deal and set about building a following. He was not even close to an overnight sensation, and it had taken him a long time to develop and prosper. Tillis was very fortunate to have arrived on the Nashville scene in the sixties. If he had been a product of modern country music, he might never have been given the time to evolve into the hot-selling star that he was destined to become. The business was more forgiving and nurturing at that time. It was also more loyal. Unlike today, the fans, country music radio, and the record labels all believed that it took time to "grow" a star.

When Pam was ten years old and spending her spare moments at the piano, Mel Tillis hit the top ten for the first time with Kapp single number 959. The year was 1968. The song that drove him there was called "Who's Julie?" Its seventeen-week ride on the charts saw the single peak at number 10. It had taken Mel thirty-one single releases over more than ten years to finally manage a modest hit. A year later he would top out at number nine with "These Lonely Hands of Mine." His first big hit wouldn't arrive until single number 36 in 1970, Mel's own remake of the hit he had written in the cookie truck for Ray Price, "Heart Over Mind."

"Heart Over Mind" had first helped establish Mel as one of Nashville's best songwriters. Now it had now given Tillis, the entertainer, the chance to be recognized as more than a background player and songwriter in Music City. He could finally look beyond small, smoky clubs that produced even smaller paychecks. Now his name was going to appear at the big shows. Mel capitalized on his newfound success by signing with Hank Williams's old label, MGM. Striking while the iron was hot, he spent even more time working on the road and in the studio than he had before.

As Mel cranked out hits like "I Ain't Never" and "Neon Rose," things continued to go downhill at home. As he admitted in his autobiography, his and Doris's relationship was simply not one built on the kind of things that caused a couple to grow closer together. In reality, this marriage seemed to be built strictly on the children. And by now, there were four kids at home with Doris. The kids may have united them, but they didn't bring the couple any closer together. In many ways, as time passed, the children were Mel and Doris's only common bond.

In 1991, when looking back at her teen years, Pam told the Country Music Association's *Close Up* magazine, "For whatever reasons, I feel that he [her father] kinda let the reins go in our family. He kind of turned it over to Mom."

As Pam considered her formative years, she showed wisdom about how and why things had turned out the way that they did.

"Both Mom and Dad were also victims of the era. Their circumstances and what they did were typical of their generation. Dad was the breadwinner. He delegated raising the family. Mama was what I call 'satellites'—women who revolve around men.

"And Dad, being a great, powerful person that he was, people tend to do that anyway. So I just think it's important for women to have their own identity. And she (Mom) didn't really get that until after they were split for a long, long time."

As she noted in her first Arista album's liner notes, Pam was very close to her mother. They had a great deal of time together with Mel on the road working as much as he was. Yet as Pam would later come to realize, there were things that her mother gave the kids, beyond her time, that created some problems.

It seemed that Mel wanted to keep a tighter rein on Pam and her siblings than Doris did. He did not want to see them spoiled. He wanted them to grow up earning what they received. Yet he was not home enough to balance his wife's more permissive influence. Essentially that is what this father/mother relationship lacked to make it a solid family unit—balance. Pam was intuitive, bright, and even as a child, a girl who deeply studied others. She recognized her mother's problems in dealing assertively with her kids and knew that Doris probably wasn't being tough enough.

"It has to do with learning to say no," Pam told *Close Up*. "And she never said no to anybody, her children, her husband."

Not saying no to Mel obviously had created the dilemma that began this marriage. Continuing to go along with his dreams and give up on her own aspirations had created an atmosphere that made Doris little more than a background player in every facet of their relationship. This fact was not wasted on Pam either. When she was later getting her own life in order, she remembered back to the tough and lonely times her mother experienced while dealing with a relationship that didn't offer much in the way of love, hope, security, or compassion.

"To a point you give as much as you can," Pam wisely told a reporter in the early nineties, "but you do need to save a little for yourself . . . I don't want to be a career woman without love in my life. But I don't want to be a person without her own dreams."

In a very real way, Pam was able to see the strengths in both her parents and somehow assimilate them into her own life. Rather than blaming her father for his lack of time and energy when it came to being a parent, she instead found the positive points in his career and learned to treasure the bits and pieces of time she did manage to get with him. While other entertainers' children often grew bitter and lashed out trying to hurt their famous parents, Pam treated Mel as if he were a doctor who simply couldn't get home from his practice to watch a recital or a ball game. She accepted that fact and moved on.

In her mother Pam seemed to recognize a woman with great potential who had been trapped by the expectations and rigid structure of the times. While Pam was able to appreciate the hours of devotion that Doris showed her children, she also wanted her mother to get out and carve her own niche in life. She didn't want to see her cheated out of the real experiences of life.

In a very real sense, the career Pam later would be driven to achieve, as well as the solid and single-minded time and devotion that she would give to her own son, was born out of the observations of her own youth. In a life that offered her all the reasons to go on television talk shows and blast her parents for not measuring up, she somehow found good role models that helped shape her own successful life. Still, as a teen, she didn't exactly have role models for a Donna Reed-type home, either.

When she finished junior high, Pam enrolled in Overton High School. Even though her father was now cranking out scores of top five hits, she was treated pretty normally. After all, she lived in Nashville—Music City—the focal point of country music, and lots of her peers' parents either worked in that business or knew people who did. And at the time, much like it had been when her father was growing up, kids did not consider country music to be the least bit cool anyway. So while the other kids at Overton were aware of who her father was, they just weren't into what he was doing. Now if Pam had had a father who was a big rock star, then it might have been different. But hey, Hank Williams, Jr. had gone to school here too, and nobody treated him any differently just because his father had been one of country music's greatest influences. So Pam's last name was neither a help nor a burden when she dealt with friends and teachers.

In school, Pam continued her music work by joining the high school band. Besides the clarinet, she dabbled with the oboe and saxophone as a member of the Bobcat marching band. While she was a solid student, Pam's greatest educational experience might have been watching other kids' families close up when she participated in slumber parties or sleep-overs. At many of these homes, she observed what other children had in the way of special and daily relationships with their dads. It was probably here that Pam first began to realize just what it was she was missing. So, while she said she understood that her father had to be gone so much and she accepted it with very little questioning, she was beginning not to like it. Like any daughter, she wanted him around more, and even Mel recognized that this was natural. He would have liked to see his kids more, too.

Missing an important element of her life may have helped to push Pam to embrace the blues as one of her favorite forms of music. She loved the emotion that was evident every time she heard a blues song. As she would later admit, listening to the blues shaped her, got into her system, created a pulse and beat all its own. She forged this blues-type emotion and feeling into everything she sang—gospel, rock, and even country. It was probably the emotional release of the blues that would carry her through years of searching and struggling as she began a pilgrimage to find her niche in the world of music and in life. Perhaps due in no small part to her environment, this was a search that began at a younger age for Pam than most of her friends.

Attempting to discover who she was through music pointed to just how much Mel's creativity fueled his daughter. In a very real sense, the void he created in Pam's life by building a successful career and being gone so much brought her something too. His songwriting, his expression of his own emotions and feelings in words and tunes, gave his daughter an outlet she really needed.

"I know most little girls want to be different things growing up," she would later say, "but I always wanted to be a singer. Seeing Daddy do it, his approach was so natural . . . like breathing. It wasn't something he ever thought about. It's like that for me, too. It's just something that has to come out."

Still, Pam would also admit that even at an early age she didn't really want to be compared to her dad. As his power and fame grew, she felt like a little twig growing up beside a huge oak tree. That was intimidating and may have been one of the reasons as she pushed deeper and deeper into her own favorite kinds of music that she pushed herself further and further away from country music.

Musicians, especially those who write much of what they sing, always look for outlets to perform. For Mel, it had been at local social and school functions. For so many others who had hit it big in country music it was church. For Pam, who had already sung on the stage of the Grand Ole Opry, it was much different. She found her venues by talking her way into performing at area clubs.

When she was fifteen, Pam played her eclectic kind of music at the Villager Club in Hillsboro Village. By telling a few stories to the management and using her last name to its full advantage, she somehow got around the fact that she was too young to be playing at such venues. She won some modest approval for her rock and blues sounds at the Villager and also had some success on talent night at Nashville's Last Chance Saloon.

Like her father during his youth, Pam would play almost anywhere that would give her a mike and a spotlight. In all honesty, Mel probably would rather have had her at home than hitting high notes in dark clubs. He knew firsthand that the nightlife could be awfully fast for anyone, much less a girl who was too young to vote or drive a car.

"I got paid in beer and the manager of the club wanted to manage me," she recalled about the time spent in the Last Chance Saloon. "Even then I knew better."

Many who came to hear the Tillis girl expected her to cover hits by the likes of Connie Smith or Patsy Cline. They were shocked to find that Pam was singing the music of Arlo Guthrie, Phoebe Snow, Hoyt Axton, and Janis Joplin. She was also listening to the Eagles, Allman Brothers, and Lynyrd Skynyrd and incorporating their sounds into her own compositions. Mel couldn't figure out where she was coming from or where she wanted to go, and he couldn't wait for her to outgrow this phase in her life. Of course, there were other things he couldn't wait for her to outgrow, too.

In his own book Mel wrote, "The older kids, Pam and Connie, were now in high school. They were bringing their share of problems home. Whatever Doris or I would tell them, they'd do just the opposite."

Besides the fact that he didn't approve of her music or the way she was acting, Mel didn't care for the "mod" way that Pam liked to dress either. He also didn't like her make-up or some of her friends. And he thought that Doris was letting Pam grow up way too fast. He was not shy about stating that he thought she was out of control, but because he was gone so much, Mel seemed unable to influence his daughter into slowing down. Some friends and associates even observed that Mel was genuinely worried that Pam might kill herself by driving recklessly or being caught at the wrong kind of party. In retrospect, Pam herself knew that she was too wild for her own good.

"Music was a saving grace for me," she told *Close Up* two decades later. "Music kept me from really messing up because I was truly a wild child."

A portion of Pam's wildness could be attributed to the times. With Vietnam brewing resentment in youth across the nation, with the country caught in the midst of the era of Woodstock and flower children, and at a time when American troops had killed college students during a protest and respected university professors were taking LSD, the world seemed to be going straight to hell. Merle Haggard was voicing the concerns of the "silent majority" with songs such as "Fightin' Side of Me." Meanwhile, the president was involved in a major scandal and assassinations had taken some of the country's most eloquent voices of reason. Some questioned if anyone would have the courage to stand up for the right things in public again. To many of the nation's youth, these days looked like the end of the world. And for many, this was a time when they decided that they were either going to enjoy this final wild ride to the fullest or search for meaning in the midst of the chaos. Unlike most, who chose to be either carnal or cerebral, Pam did both.

While listening to rock standards like the mournful "American Pie," the beautiful "Heart Of Gold," or the bombastic preaching of "You're So Vain," she was riding out the moments with the annoying but seemingly harmless age-old rituals of youth. She was experimenting with booze and fast cars. She was never going to win any Daughters of the American Revolution awards this way, but she thought she was having a good time and wasn't too concerned about the fact that she was worrying her parents sick. In retrospect, someone should have cracked down on her, but no one did. So she partied on.

At about the same time that Mel was tearing up the charts with his second biggest hit up until that moment, "Sawmill," Pam's wild teenage ride came to a quick and almost fatal stop. On an evening when she and a group of her friends had been partying way too long and hard, she had to pay for her wicked ways. She now freely admits that she was being stupid. She had had far too much to drink and had still gotten in the car. While the events that followed seemed more surreal than real, she suddenly found her face flying toward the car's windshield. The force of impact would shatter the glass, cut her skin to shreds, and practically tear her face off. Those who viewed the car wondered how she could have survived. Those who saw what the crash had done to Pam's face wondered how anyone could ever put her back together again.

When the doctors originally finished sewing her face back together, her once beautiful smile and sweet expression had been replaced by a horrid road map of lines and scars. She was alive, she would be all right physically, but she now looked more like a freak than a potential prom date.

Mel would explain to those who asked about Pam's condition and the wreck that it had ended up "smashing her [Pam's] pretty face flat." Even though it was a club that she had never asked to join, suddenly Pam found herself coupled to Hank Williams, Jr. in another way. Now not only were they the offspring of country music stars who had attended the same high school, but they had both broken every bone in their faces in tragic accidents. They were also both lucky to be alive.

Just as Mel had not hidden in a room because of his stuttering, Pam didn't retreat either. She continued to go out, to work on her music, to appear in clubs. Even in the midst of several trips to Los Angeles to begin the process of having this country's best cosmetic surgeons fix her mangled face, she made the rounds looking for places to play.

"She dropped by several times and played with my rock band," remembers Rick King, now the director for Louise Mandrell's Spellbound band. "We were playing at a place in Murfreesboro called the Solution. It must have been pretty soon after her wreck, because at that time Pam's face was still messed up. Yet it didn't keep her from getting up in front of people and singing with us. I thought she really handled the questions people asked about her scars very well. In spite of everything, she seemed to have a really good self-concept."

Yet any high school girl who had been cut up as badly as Pam had must have suffered a great deal. In 1993 she told *Country Fever Magazine,* "I looked terrible for so long . . . I was an ugly duckling in school, real bad." She hated her school pictures and at that time in her life it must have been frustrating to have to go through so much surgery over such a long period of time to fix the damage that had been done.

Yet she had her father's example to fall back on. He had achieved things in school even when others had looked upon him as a freak. He had used his obvious problems to his advantage. He hadn't run and he hadn't hid. He had pushed forward when others wanted to hold him back. If Mel could overcome so much, if he could show such great courage, why couldn't his daughter?

Even as she flew back and forth to the West Coast to let Hollywood's finest work on her face, Pam stepped up her performing schedule. Many of her best shows were in what most of those who made up the largest core of country music fans—the Bible-belt crowd—would have considered dives. One of the best known and most respectable of these was Nashville's Exit/In.

The Exit/In was a dark, smoky downtown venue, usually filled with men and women who were often drinking away the woes of long, hard days. The bands that normally played this hot spot were pure country. Pam was singing her type of rock and blues. And while she was still underage, those who watched her, as well as those who hired her, either didn't know or didn't care. A lot of them did like the hard edge of her music, though. During a time when almost everyone in Nashville was conforming to one of two different styles, she was different. She was not a Mel Tillis clone; as a matter of fact, she didn't sound like anybody who was then working in Music City. There was a kind of West Coast, as well as a Mississippi Delta blues feel about her. While she was winning small pockets of applause, many, including her father, wanted to know why she was trying to shock Music City with this alternative type of music rather than taking advantage of her connections. Why didn't she just trade off her name and go the way it seemed she was meant to go?

Maybe the most ironic thing about this time in her life was that Pam seemed to be far more patient with those who wanted to know what happened to her face than with those who wanted to know why she wasn't doing country music. This again reminded some people of her father. Mel came into Nashville when everybody, including stars like Marty Robbins, were trying to go rockabilly. Yet he stubbornly kept doing his shuffle-beat, honky-tonk thing. He didn't throw away his fiddle players and held on to his twang. And everyone wondered what in the heck he was doing. He could laugh and joke about his stuttering, but his music was something he didn't joke about. He took it seriously.

Even though it was a different style of music, Pam was doing the same thing. She would always answer that she was doing what she wanted to do. And in Pam's mind it was a whole lot better than working as a Stutterette in her dad's band. She had tried that and found it not only unchallenging, but somewhat demeaning. It might have been a shortcut to some type of fame, but Pam thought if she could make her own breaks and find her own way it would be a whole lot more satisfying. And as she graduated from high school and gave up her days of innocent youth, she was more than ready to try.

Pam would later tell writer Sally Schloss in *Tune-In Magazine,* "Look, you're 16, you're 18—you don't know what the hell's going on here." Of course, as she began to look down the road to her adult years, she could take comfort in the fact that the entire country didn't seem to know what the hell was going on either.

Chapter Three

The mid-seventies was a time like no other. While most periods in history are an echo of another from a few decades before, this decade stood by itself—from fashion fads to movies that gave up entertainment values in order to try to make important statements about every phase of life. From sitcoms that pushed the envelope of taste by presenting lead characters who represented bigotry and narrow-mindedness, to music that went from mindless dance-driven techno-rock to syrupy love ballads. The war in Vietnam, the civil rights movement, the burning of many of America's inner cities, the rise of the moral majority and the blossoming of the flower child movement had enlarged the generation gap to near-record proportions. While parents were downsizing their cars, worrying about the Arab oil embargo and trying to protect the sanctity of home and family, kids were purchasing black lights, dancing in disco clubs, joining Greenpeace, and preaching the virtues of free love. Confusion reigned, and the consistency of change and the stability of slowly evolving tastes had been tossed out the window for a frantic, psychedelic ride. For most what seemed frightening was that Andy Warhol's views on the meaning of life were a lot closer to being accepted as fact than Richard Nixon's.

Yet in a real way, Nixon may have represented the

America of the era far better than anyone else. Like the fallen leader, the country was paranoid. No one seemed to trust anyone else anymore, and while there were more opportunities for women and minorities in most facets of the business world, there was also a large and deepening rift developing between those who had and those who wanted to have. It was a strange time, when strange people achieved a certain level of fame and influence, and as always, the nation's instabilities, as well as its hopes and uncertainties, were represented in the arts as well as politics.

As Pam Tillis graduated from high school, she couldn't miss the wind of change that was sweeping the nation, even the Bible-belt South. A Southerner who raised peanuts, listened to country music and proudly admitted it, who wore blue jeans and went by a nickname was actually being considered as a serious presidential candidate. Logic somehow seemed to follow that if Jimmy Carter could smile his way into the world's most important office, then Dolly Parton thought the time was right to jiggle her way to stardom in Hollywood. And Dolly really thought that she was ready to take popular music and the movies by storm. Shockingly, like Carter, she would even grant an interview to *Playboy*. This was a long way from selling Breeze and singing gospel standards on the *Porter Wagoner Show*. Everyone in Nashville was talking about Dolly, and Pam had to notice that the Tennessee blonde was making a splash in a bigger pond than Music City. But could she really open up the tightly closed world of country music to accept acts with broader appeal? Or as Dolly might put it, to even accept broads running their own careers!

Joe DiMaggio might have been gone, but at least in the world of sports the fans had someone to hang onto and cheer for whom they knew would never disillusion them. Everyone was calling O. J. Simpson the next "James Brown," and the halfback was on his way to becoming one of the first high-profile black commercial pitchmen. In the world's eye, this was an all-American if there ever was one.

Of course, while Pam might care little about the Juice, even when he was running through airports, on television she couldn't have missed the impact of *Saturday Night Live*. After all, if Pam was known by her friends for anything, it was her great sense of humor. And if there was ever a show that was so quickly and religiously embraced by the baby boomers who loved to laugh like young Miss Tillis, it was this late night blend of humor and satire. High school and college kids regularly memorized the routines of stars who overnight had gone from small comedy clubs to become some of the biggest names in entertainment. Yet *SNL*'s success also showed the growing chasm between country music and other forms of artistic expression. In the past there had been a link between the humor presented on the stage of the Grand Ole Opry and the material on the television variety shows of such stars as Jack Benny or George Burns. The humor of Gracie Allen and that of Opry comedian Rod Brasfield hadn't been all that different. Yet finding the common ground between the Opry and *SNL* was all but impossible. The gang who loved Chevy Chase was probably going to dismiss the punch lines of Minnie Pearl. Then again, a lot of those in Nashville were dismissing a large and vital segment of the punch that was now a part of mainstream music too, so the trade-off seemed fair.

How strange was the music industry as a whole? In 1976, the Bellamy Brothers were a rock group who scored a number one in May with "Let Your Love Flow." It seemed bizarre that a duo that would later have such impact on the country music charts could compete at that time with acts such as the Bee Gees, KC and the Sunshine Band, Wild Cherry, and Rick Dees and His Cast of Idiots, not to mention the more middle-of-the-road pop stars such as Diana Ross, Barry Manilow, and Chicago. Yet such was the musical confusion that was so accepted during this time. In a world that must have seemed completely mad to many who had survived the Depression and World War II, a bloated Elvis was playing before packed houses of screaming grandmothers and their orgasmic daughters and granddaughters, and C. W. McCall was hitting the top of the rock charts with a blatantly country ode, "Convoy." What in the heck was going on?

While the kids and "hip" jetsetters were grooving to "The Love Machine," country music found itself in the midst of something called "The Outlaw Movement." Waylon Jennings, Willie Nelson, Johnny Paycheck, and a few others had traded in their Nudie suits, let their hair grow, left Music City for Texas, and had become the leaders in a hillbilly counter-culture movement. With songs like "Good-Hearted Woman," they were suddenly pushing a new younger sound to an audience that had been used to hearing country music evolve slowly. A young blind singer, Ronnie Milsap, was also shaking things up by resurrecting the rock sounds of the fifties, while an old rocker, Conway Twitty, was singing about sexual matters that made many listeners blush. The old-time guard must have been having a heart attack when Jim Ed Brown and Helen Cornelius ruled the charts with a number that seemed to embrace premarital sex, "I Don't Want to Have to Marry You." And if that wasn't shocking enough, a black man, Charlie Pride, and a hispanic, Freddy Fender, were displacing Ray Price and Marty Robbins as the voices of real country music.

Surprisingly, in the midst of all of these revolutionary developments, Pam's father was calmly doing his own traditional thing. Seemingly unconcerned about country music's multiple-personality complex, or the strange mood of the country as a whole, Mel kept working his ever-growing crowds with corn-fed humor and shuffle-beat music. Most of the rest of the world might have been trying to cash in on the latest fad, but he wasn't. He didn't want fifteen minutes of fame, he wanted staying power. Mel believed that the best way to do this was to keep his twin fiddles, his country-cut suits, and his well-worn one-liners. Others urged him to get a bit more progressive, but he insisted he knew what his fans really wanted. By fall, he would discover just how good his instincts had been.

Around Nashville in clubs where she performed, Pam seemed to want to try every new style that was rushing out of the gate except her father's brand of music. With her voice maturing, her fever to write making her ever more expressive, and the scars on her face rapidly being wiped away by the skilled hands of Los Angeles's finest cosmetic surgeons, she was gaining more and more confidence in herself and her music. Even though she showed such great promise, her family didn't want her to charge right into the business. They seemed to believe that an opportunity to widen her world through higher learning was in order. At a time when so many in her generation were dropping out, she was dropping into the University of Tennessee in Knoxville. As it turned out, the Volunteers wouldn't have her for long.

Within days of landing on the stately historic campus, Pam joined a band. Even though many naturally figured that with a Tillis in the mix, the group would lean to a Nashville-based sound, the group played more rock than two-step dance music. Yet there was still a bit of the country influence in their sound. The band's members probably had no idea just how close they were to being on the cutting edge of country music's future either. A few years down the road Charlie Daniels, Hank Williams, Jr., and Alabama would wake up Music City by merging country and rock into something the industry would call "dixie-rock." And what an impact it would make. Doors would fly open for acts that had once been excluded from the genre. Through those doors would charge not only dozens of hot new groups and singers, but millions of young fans. For performers like Pam, it would be a God-send, but in 1976 no one would have believed that it would ever happen.

"The first week on campus I signed up for a rock-and-roll group,'' Pam later explained to the press, ''and then my classes. Later, I sang for something called the High Country Swing Band; we did a mix of camp jug band music and country rock.''

From her first day on campus, Pam picked up where she had left off in Nashville. School was going to take a back seat to music. If she had choice of playing guitar and trading licks with a friend or going to class, the strings would win out over the classroom every time. Music was fast becoming the primary focus of her life.

''My major in college was music and partying,'' Pam still freely admits. ''And for a while, I was in a duet with another singer named Ashley Cleveland. (Cleveland would go on to do a stint with John Hiatt's touring band and even swing a deal with Atlantic records as a rocker.) I just couldn't get enough of singing. It was a way for me to get out of myself, to express who I really was.'' And she was expressing herself with some other pretty talented people.

During her brief stay at UT, Pam might have gained little in the way of ''book learning,'' but she did grow up musically. After embracing a sound that was somewhat like the Eagles, she gave up on college and returned home. Thanks to events that were transpiring in her father's camp, she had a job waiting for her in Music City.

In October, Mel Tillis walked onto the center of the hallowed Grand Ole Opry stage and accepted the award for Country Music's ''Entertainer of the Year.'' In a very real sense, Mel was riding alone, proudly holding onto the spirit of real country music. The others who had been nominated for this most hallowed of all country music awards were Dolly Parton, now trying to make it in Los Angeles and on the pop charts, Waylon Jennings and Willie Nelson, the leaders of the Austin, Texas-based ''Outlaw Movement,'' and Ronnie Milsap, a modern-day country music rockabilly pop singer. When Mel's name was called, the country music establishment was exuberant.

To begin to understand just what Mel's winning meant

to Nashville, one has to look back only one year. In 1975, when Charlie Rich opened up the envelope and silently read the name of that year's "Entertainer of the Year" choice, rather than inform the crowd, he had pulled out a lighter and set the card on fire. He was simply not going to acknowledge that pop/folk star John Denver, a man with no Nashville ties, had won the CMA's greatest honor. Now with Mel's victory, the country music community felt as if they had taken their music back from the anti-establishment, West Coast, folk-rock driven crowd. Many believed that this would end the revolt of the Outlaws, as well as those who were forsaking country music for the opportunity to make high dollars in pop.

As much as it meant to country music, Mel, who had just earned his second number-one single with "Good Woman Blues," knew it meant a great deal more to him. He had finally earned complete acceptance. He could now really move on with his life and maybe even cut back a little on the time he spent working. After almost two decades of ignoring everything but his career, he could now take stock of his private life and put things in order.

One of the things he did was split with his wife and marry another woman who had been a part of his life and business for some time. He would also begin to travel in select "star" crowds that included Burt Reynolds and Robert Redford. He would make movies. And in the midst of all of these exciting things, he would welcome his college-dropout daughter back into his fold by offering her a job with his Sawgrass Music Publishing company.

So when Pam returned to Nashville, she didn't have to wait to continue her music. Drawing living expenses as a writer was a good way to make up for the fact that she was often working for free making music in small clubs. Even though her sound was completely different from anything her father was doing, she quickly realized that she was always being compared to Mel. Almost everyone kept telling her that she was supposed to sing country like her dad. That is what the fans expected and in some cases demanded. Now that her father was the "Entertainer of the Year" and more in the spotlight than ever, she had to realize that Music City was simply not going to give "Pam Tillis, the rock act" a fair shake. So it didn't take long for Pam to figure out that her talents and her taste in music weren't going to get much positive attention in a city that didn't have much time for country stars like Waylon Jennings and Willie Nelson.

The boots Pam had to fill were awfully large and it didn't take a genius to note that the other star offspring around town weren't having much luck filling the boots of their parents either. Hank Jr. wasn't on top of the world yet. Conway's kids were trying and hadn't made it. Neither had Marty Robbins or Ernest Tubb's sons. And those acts had all tried to make it in their fathers' genres. They hadn't wanted to rebel like Pam did.

Pam felt that she was just as expressive and creative as Mel, but she also felt stifled by having to do things his way. Like most teens, she wanted to stretch her wings and see what her limits were. She appreciated that her father had worked hard to earn his level of respect and success, but the kind of music he was doing was not what was in her soul. The two of them had such different taste.

Mel thought he had the answer to their difference of opinion. Pam just needed to change hers. If she sang and wrote straight country, the old-fashioned kind like he sang, then she could have her dream of working the spotlight in much bigger venues than tiny Nashville clubs. He thought that she would definitely play before a higher class of people. Yet as always, Pam had her own ideas, and listening to Mel's advice wasn't on her agenda at that time. Still, she was beginning to be caught up by the opportunity that he had given her. The job at his publishing company was exciting. Working with top-flight songwriters was opening up a whole new world to the young songwriter.

Pam would later say, "I'd gotten a serious songwriting bug back then. I wanted to know how songwriting really was done. I concentrated on the craft, especially lyrics. That's where I learned about structure and style."

And that paid off as others began to note the potential of Pam's work. One of the first was Barbara Fairchild.

In 1976, Barbara was just past the peak of her career. Four years before she had scored a monster hit with "The Teddy Bear Song." Since that time, she had charted in the top ten two other times. Pam's original, "I'll Meet You on the Other Side of the Morning" would become a top 100 hit for Barbara Fairchild. This was an exiting first for Tillis, but just another failed effort for Fairchild. They were two acts headed in different ways. Barbara would eventually follow Mel to Branson and rebuild her career in the Missouri hills two decades later. Pam would wander around before making her mark in the very place that was now stifling her growth.

The fact was that while being recorded was great, Pam was not gearing up her career to write songs for other folks. She was even keeping a majority of her good stuff in hopes that someday she could cut the originals herself. So while having a hit song recorded by an outside act might earn her respect as a writer, what she really wanted was a record deal of her own. But she didn't want one that her now powerful father could whip up in a hurry, only to find herself trapped into singing Mel's kind of country music. She wanted to earn her own deal where she could do her own thing.

One of Music City's finest producers, Jimmy Bowen, noticed her and encouraged her. Bowen was not just impressed with her writing, he liked the direction Pam was going with music. Bowen probably recognized that young Tillis was taking her own music in a direction that country music was destined to grow. She had a sound that was going to evolve into an important player in the marketplace in a few years. For this change to be realized, first the industry had to shift that way, and secondly, Pam had to mature and refine her sound so that she could be ready to capitalize on her talents and vision. Bowen knew that both things would take a while.

Unlike her father, whose advice she usually ignored, Pam listened to Bowen. She tried to grow in the direction he felt would benefit her most. When he encouraged her to listen to certain writers and certain acts and take her music a bit in that direction, she gave it a shot. Jimmy was a mentor she respected and admired. He genuinely seemed ready to help her come into her own.

Pam would have been smart to continue to work with her father, even go out on the road with him and sing a song or two as a part of his band, keep working with Bowen and other established Nashville movers and shakers, and use the Tillis name and contacts to get herself a country music record deal. Pam might have landed a hit or two in the process. But it wasn't what Pam wanted to do.

Much to Mel's disappointment, even after working with his country writers at Sawgrass Music for some time, his daughter was still largely unimpressed with the direction that country music was headed. She didn't have any ambition to do shuffle-beat, outlaw, or honky-tonk. Even Ronnie Milsap's middle of the road, retro-rockabilly style was too tame for Pam. She was in love with the sound of the Allman Brothers Band, Phoebe Snow, and the Eagles. And while at some point these influences would help to shape a new harder-edged sound in country music—the sound that Jimmy Bowen must have sensed was coming—radio at the time was being driven by the likes of George Jones and Tammy Wynette's "Golden Rings," "El Paso City" by Marty Robbins, and "I'll Get Over You" by Crystal Gayle. None of these sounds appealed to Pam's style and she saw no place for herself in Music City.

Pam wasn't alone. Dozens of talented pickers and singers who had grown up around or migrated to Nashville were finding few places where they could really express themselves. While the nation may have been leaning toward the left of center, Music City was still very much pushing toward the right. Even the area clubs offered few outlets for rock music. It was obvious to Pam that to do "her thing," to gain an identity other than as Mel's daughter, she was going to have to go somewhere else. Like thousands of other young people of her day, when faced with the choice of going someplace to "find herself," Pam chose San Francisco.

There was little arguing that this city by the Bay was one of the most beautiful in the world. San Francisco was also a place where freedom of expression was not just accepted, it was almost worshipped. Here was the region the original flower children called home. Here was a city where drugs flowed freely and people used them openly. Here was a place where homosexuals were allowed to speak their minds and practice their lifestyle. With an atmosphere as open as any in the United States, San Francisco seemed to be the perfect city for young and talented musicians to find themselves.

At nineteen, Pam was still in many ways a kid growing up. Rebellious yet friendly, respectful yet not wanting much to do with the older generation's viewpoints, Mel's daughter was anxious to escape every label that anyone could hang on her. With that in mind when she decided to move, Pam got together with a bunch of itinerant musicians and headed out.

In all honesty, the heyday of San Francisco "mod" youth had come and gone. Most of the flower children and hippies had run out of money or gotten a bit long in the tooth and returned to the real world. Yet that didn't keep Pam from trying to make her mark as a "hippie-come-lately." For a young girl from Nashville, even one who had worked the smoky clubs and partied long and hard, this was a brand new world! Besides seeing a place that was radically different from her home and enjoying one of the most beautiful cities anywhere, Pam soon discovered another luxury—few seemed to know who Mel Tillis was and no one judged her even if they did. She was free to do whatever she wanted musically.

"We called ourselves the Pam Tillis Band," she later explained as she looked back on those carefree days, "and we all lived together commune-style on a barge in Sausalito. It was really inspiring to me, being nineteen years old and on my own for the first time." Included in this group was John Cipollina from Quick Silver Message Service, and his brother Mario, who later toured with Huey Lewis and the News.

Mario was still working his way up the musical ladder too, but he would find success much quicker than the band's namesake and lead singer. By the early eighties, he and Huey Lewis were charting consistently with a rock sound that was forged in many of the same clubs where Pam was working on her own style.

After a short while and a few member changes, the Pam Tillis Band became Freeflight, which as the name might suggest, was a very free form of jazz, rock, and whatever else Pam and her buddies came across. They were literally trying to play anything and then, if they liked it, merge it into their sound. The ensemble made something of a name for itself in the Bay Area. But it didn't make a whole lot of money. As the months dragged by, Pam turned more and more to jazz. While this was not a music that was "happening" financially, it was a creative art form that allowed rich expression. Young Tillis loved this freedom.

Pam would later say that it was singing jazz that "freed me vocally, and it made me know that I could do a lot more with my voice than I grew up thinking was possible." Maybe it was because of jazz that Pam quit trying to imitate many of her musical influences and began to develop her own style. As different as she had seemed before she had left Nashville, now she was embracing a vocal style and phrasing that was really setting her apart from what was happening in Music City. Those who liked her said that Pam Tillis didn't sing like anyone else. Those who didn't like her would say the same thing! This unique new identity would prove to be both a curse and a blessing when Pam later carved out her career in country music.

"We were a real arty band, which is probably why we couldn't get a deal," Pam later said about her jazz ensemble. Of course she also admitted that "we didn't make any sense . . . it was nuts." Maybe that was another reason they didn't get a record deal. Yet in a very real sense, that is the way jazz is. And even though most folks, especially her father, thought she was crazy, she was having a great deal of fun singing it.

By 1978, Freeflight had disbanded and Pam began singing with another group, The Ramsey Lewis Trio. All the while her father would call and tell her, "Come on home. You're better than any of the girl singers around here. You can make it country music if you will just give it a try."

Mel may have been right. Doors just might have opened if Pam had been willing to come back, work with a solid country music producer, and do the kind of stuff that was being recorded by the genre's new acts. Producers such as Tom Collins were churning out what many considered country music bubble-gum music. But this version of "country lite" was producing hits and they were making big money. About the same time that Pam was singing jazz in the Bay Area, Collins even took his secretary, gave her formula songs and heavy production and turned her into a star. Her name was Sylvia and songs like "Tumbleweed," "Drifter," and later, "Nobody," were putting her high on the charts.

Another Collins singer, Barbara Mandrell, was making even higher grades. While many of Barbara's songs were just as formulaic as the others Tom gave his stable of singers to record, the small blonde had far more talent than folks like Sylvia. She was a solid, seasoned, dynamic entertainer. Joining Barbara and Sylvia were a long list of other hit-producing women including Crystal Gayle (Loretta Lynn's half-sister), Dottie West, Margo Smith, and Janie Frickie. Hence, there seemed to be a place for Pam in the industry if she was willing to conform, but everyone who knew her knew that even if she did come back home, she wasn't going to play the game by anything but her own rules. Ultimately, it wasn't the fact that Music City was looking for new female singers that led Pam back to Nashville. Nor was it because she had grown tired of singing jazz. It was a relationship that brought Mel's daughter back to her father, not a desire to come back to Nashville and get into country music.

Not long after arriving in San Francisco, Pam had met Rick Mason. Mason was a good-looking Iowan who was also on the West Coast trying to find himself. He was an artist type, a singer/painter who was trying out his wings for the first time. Soon the two became a pair, getting into the faddish new age West Coast habits of herbs, natural doctoring, and a hippie-like lifestyle. Eventually they decided that they were in love and got married. Mel soon got the word that he not only had a son-in-law, but he was going to become a grandfather.

The newly married Mel offered the couple one of his homes in Ashland City. Once again, he gave Pam a job earning a weekly draw as a songwriter for Sawgrass Music. Mel was more concerned about the fact that the young couple wanted to have their child the old-fashioned way—no hospital, no drugs, no state-of-the-art care—than anything else going on in Pam's life at this time. Yet in spite of Mel's worried mind, when the time came, and a son, Ben Asher Mason, was born, Pam and her baby survived just fine. Everything considered, life was looking up. Mel had his daughter back in Nashville, and while she was not a bit more settled and not much more mature than when she left, she had married a pretty good country boy and the singer had a grandson. Then, just three weeks after Ben was born, Pam and Rick broke up. Their brief marriage was history.

Needing a bit more help than could be provided even from across town, Pam and Ben moved in with Mel and his new wife. It would give the singer an opportunity to bond much sooner with his grandson than he ever had with any of his and Doris's children. It would also give Mel and his oldest daughter a chance to get to know each other a little better, too. With Ben, they finally had something besides creativity and the Tillis's stubborn streak in common. It was a good place to start and something wonderful to build upon.

Chapter Four

In the mid-eighties when Pam Tillis and soon-to-be husband Bob DiPiero penned the words to "Melancholy Child," they knew that they were piecing together an autobiographical quilt. A series of phrases that represented Pam's series of phases. Certainly she had been a restless child trapped in a world where she felt confined, and this had to have been frustrating for the young woman trying so hard to spread her musical wings and fly in her own direction—to chart her own course. Yet at the same time that she was bound by her family name, there was also a great deal of personal freedom, as well as access to Music City, when you were the daughter of Mel Tillis. Doors that could be opened for Pam were ones to which a commoner would never be given the key. These were the privileges which the oldest daughter of the Country Music Association's Entertainer of the Year could obtain by default. They were the spoils that went along with being at the far edge of the spotlight. By and large, Pam passed on these. Living off her father's fame didn't appeal to her. Pam wanted to test herself on her own merits.

Still, she did allow Daddy to arrange for her to obtain a job as a writer for his publishing company, and against her better judgment, she also accepted a place in his band. Mel thought it would be perfect to have his daughter on stage singing harmonies with his "Stutterettes." It seemed from the first that Pam knew this was not a good idea. If she had her life to live over again, this is one place she would probably never stop.

Young Miss Tillis was simply not into the honky-tonk sound and cornball humor that drove her father's career. She wasn't a "Coca-Cola Cowgirl," rather she was a jazz-inspired "rock-gut" rocker. It was hard to be Janis Joplin in spangles and boots. As she admitted when she wrote about her life experiences in "Melancholy Child," she was unsettled. She had to be challenged and she had to be growing. At this time in country music, she felt as if she was stuck in a rut. There was no place for her to grow or go. And in comparing her sound and look to those who were selling records at the time, she was probably right.

The women who were emerging as forces on the country music charts of the era were a great deal different from Pam. Crystal Gayle was a soft-pop stylist who took middle-of-the-road compositions and gave them just enough twang to become country hits. Gayle was really much like a white Dionne Warwick. She wasn't defining moments or hitting notes with a new hard edge, she wasn't taking the genre in a radical new direction, she was simply taking a formula and using it to make the cash registers ring. Almost anyone could quickly learn the tunes to her songs, but few felt passionately about either the lyrics or the singer. Crystal, unlike her sister Loretta Lynn, wasn't expanding the role of women in the industry.

Charly McClain, a Memphis belle, was using an Epic contract to project a new sexuality in country music. While she was producing hits, she seemed to be a performer who didn't believe in what she was doing or selling. Like Gayle, there seemed to be little passion in her music. Pam believed that music couldn't "happen" without passion.

Sylvia was manufactured in this same passionless mold. Her music was catchy and cute, but not driving or significant. Her stablemate at Tom Collins's studios, Barbara Mandrell, had begun her career with a real edge (her first real hit, "The Midnight Oil," represented the first single where a woman had willingly cheated on her man), but had now largely given up her R&B influences and had emerged as "America's Sweetheart" with singles like "I Was Country When Country Wasn't Cool."

In Pam's mind, country music at this time simply wasn't cool. The only real hope that she could point to, the one person who might restore the passion to the genre was Roseanne Cash. Her music spoke about emotions, about pain and anguish. She seemed really to feel what she was doing and it was reflected in her voice. In her musical world, genuine expression mattered. Yet this second-generation performer was certainly in the minority and a large part of the country music establishment was trying to ignore her. In some ways, Cash was looked upon a bit like Ms. Tillis, a square peg trying to fit into a round hole. This perception and the way that it confined Pam's music and its spirit was probably one of the reasons Pam didn't last very long as a "Stutterette."

She would later explain it to reporters simply as a case of two generations and two talents heading in different directions with far different goals. "I was in a real rebellious stage," Pam admitted, "and our egos kind of clashed. We're both strong-willed sorts . . . that's one thing I got from him. Pat and Debbie we're not."

Another thing that might have gotten on Mel's nerves and caused the split was that Pam was always finishing his sentences. She seemed to know what he was going to say, and when he began to stutter, she would simply chime in with what he was trying to utter. It was something that she had done all of her life, but in public it ruined a bit of the Tillis charm. Folks wanted to give Mel a break and let him speak for himself. Pam simply didn't have time to wait.

A decade later she told writer Alan Sculley of *Music Monthly,* "Sometimes he (Mel) felt like any parent would.

He felt like his hands were tied. He wanted to help me, but I wouldn't let him. And it drove him crazy sometimes, you know, because for a while there, it did not look like I was going to make it. It took so long, and he was just about to give up."

Just like Pam was impatient with her father's speech problem, Mel was impatient with Pam's need to try something other than home cooking. He knew that she belonged in country music and he felt she should know that, too!

But at this time Pam wasn't about to follow in her father's footsteps. And there was just as much logic saying she shouldn't as demanding that she should. Over the years, a number of famous offspring of country music stars had tried their hands on the big stage only to have the spotlight turned off and the audience gone before they ever got to the main show. Merle Haggard's son had tried. So had Marty Robbins's kid. Sure, a name could work for you, but it could work against you, too.

It had been said for several years that Louise Mandrell was one of Nashville's most talented acts. Some argued that she had far more talent than her sister Barbara. But she hadn't been able to see that talent fully realized because she had the same name as a CMA "Entertainer of the Year." Her record label had once even had Louise record a disco number to try to break the tie between the siblings, but it hadn't worked. She was still looked upon as a novelty act, just someone following in the tracks of someone more famous. That prospect didn't seem to appeal to Pam.

Even though she was no longer on the road with him, Pam still wrote songs for Mel's company. When the writing was slow, from time to time she even tried working in the real world. She signed on with Avon and attempted to sell cosmetics to friends and family. It was obvious from the beginning that she was hardly her generation's Mary Kay Ash. Pam also worked as a waitress for a short time. She describes her exploits at this time in her life in terms that sound more like a good plot for a network situation comedy than a manual for diner work. "I was the world's worst waitress," she admitted. The best tip she probably ever received was to "get back into music," and leave the waiting on tables to folks who were a bit more skilled in such things.

From every unsuccessful job that Pam had, she took away something of importance with her. She noted the plight of ordinary folks just trying to get by. She sensed the dreams and goals of common people and the loneliness of lives which seemed to be spinning rapidly and going nowhere. Working real jobs in the real world would someday inspire songs with which real people could identify. She knew firsthand the people who would someday buy her music, and more importantly, she had a bond with them. She did this on her own by taking a step away from living off her dad and his fame and looking to make it on her own.

Back in the studio, Pam the songwriter began turning out product that sounded more and more polished. Working with the best was now paying off in the quality of the final product. More often than not, she recorded the demos for her own material, and the industry began to take note of her voice and her style. In the early eighties, Pam's original songs began to get recorded by the likes of hot new singers such as Janie Fricke.

Pam was getting together with Janie at just the right time for both of them. Even though neither knew it at the time, in some ways the two shared some mutual musical roots. Janie had been born on a farm in Indiana to a family of musicians. She had sung jingles in college and migrated to Nashville after trying her talents in rock and folk music on the West Coast. After landing a job as a receptionist, she had worked her way into demo sessions. Soon she was the most sought after back-up vocalist in Music City. Her voice became so well known that even the general public began to pick her out on Conway Twitty and Tanya Tucker releases. Capitalizing on that success, Columbia signed her as a solo act and Janie began to produce a string of hits including a number one duet with Charlie Rich, "On My Knees." Fricke was hot and getting hotter and a chance to get on one of her albums was a big deal for any new writer.

Besides Fricke, Dan Seals took note and recorded one of Pam's tunes. Seals had even deeper musical roots than Pam Tillis. His brother Jim was one-half of the Seals and Crofts team. His brother Eddie would land with Eddie and Joe. His brother Chuck was a great songwriter who penned "Crazy Arms." The other two Seals brothers would turn out all right too. Troy would become a top songwriter and Brady would gain fame down the road as a member of Little Texas.

Like Janie Fricke, Dan Seals had come to country music after a stint in pop. Starting with local Texas bands, he met and toured with John Ford Coley as England Dan & John Ford Coley and moved to Nashville. He later broke up with Coley and jumped back to Los Angeles. There he spun his wheels, lost many of his possessions and much of his past earnings to the IRS, and finally migrated over to country music. He was plying his trade as a male vocalist for Liberty in the early 1980s when he came upon some of Pam's demos.

Joining Fricke and Seals in cutting some of Tillis's stuff was Barbara Fairchild, who was now riding toward the end of her recording career. Yet as exciting as it would have been for a young songwriter to have landed a few cuts with some of Nashville's hottest new talents and one long-recognized contributor, Pam was probably much more enthused when Gloria Gaynor and Rebbie Jackson cut her stuff.

Gaynor was a New Jersey disco queen who had wowed audiences in clubs across the East Coast. Discovered in New York's Wagon Wheel, she probably should get the credit for creating disco music. Still, her biggest hit, 1979's "I Will Survive," would have been a top-notch effort in any musical format. She would cut Pam's "When I Get

Around to It'' as a dance number. Though it would not make the charts, it would be requested many times by Gloria's intensely loyal fans at live gigs.

Rebbie Jackson was another prized convert to the younger Tillis's music. Rebbie was one of Michael's older sisters. Like most members of the Jackson family, she was attempting to carve out her own career. Columbia had given her a contract, but other than going into the studio to lay down one of Pam's tunes, she would do very little with it.

Pam didn't have to be too dismayed over these two new acts' failure to produce a real hit. Because the two had recorded her, she was now being noticed in the black and R&B circles. This could only lead to better contacts and a chance at a real charting record down the road. It all came together when Pam's songwriting gained real soul—enough to impress the Pointer Sisters. The siblings gave Pam her first moderate hit with *Dare Me*.

As Pam's songwriting took on a more R&B feel, she landed even more cuts in pop, disco, and rock music. Soul singers such as Dorothy Morrie and Bettye LaVette discovered her. So did Conway Twitty.

It should have come as no surprise that Conway quickly recognized Pam's talents when others in country music wondered just what kind of statement she was trying to make. Twitty had grown up with the black blues he had heard along the Mississippi. He had sung it during his early days as a rockabilly act. And he continued to listen to it now as he searched for new release material. Conway held that country music had a lot of soul and was deep in blues. To prove his convictions, he often recorded music by writers from outside Music City. More often than not, these attempts worked and led to hits such as ''Rest Your Love on Me,'' written by Barry Gibb of the Bee Gees; ''Slow Hand,'' a Pointer Sisters smash, Bette Midler's unforgettable ''The Rose''; the Eagles' ''Heartache Tonight''; and ''Three Times a Lady'' by the Commodores. Unfortunately for Pam, few other Music City acts of the time felt the same way as Conway did. By and large, they wanted their country straightforward and with few risks.

When Pam wasn't in the studio, she could often be found in small clubs fronting for a top-forty white R&B band. With a raw sound that blended so many of the different musical elements she had heard in San Francisco, Pam was in heaven when she showed her stuff to the small but usually enthusiastic crowds.

"The whole show was choreographed," she later recalled. "I felt like a Tina Turner. I was terrific!" Those who saw her and gave her a real chance usually agreed. And boy was she different. Mel was loved for his understated style, but nothing was understated about Pam. From her driving bass beat to her wild clothes and hair, she was "out front and out there!"

Lonnie Webb, one of Barbara Mandrell's Do-Rites, now a producer with TNN, agreed with the singer's assessment of her own talent. "She was a rocker, and she was good. I knew she was Mel's daughter, but she was going for a far different audience at that time. Folks were talking about her!"

The audience she was attracting scared her dad almost as much as her music did. Pam told *People* magazine, "When he [Mel] saw me, he was horrified. My daddy doesn't necessarily understand the kind of music I do." With lyrics that included "She's obscene in all the right places," this seemed understandable.

Mel would tell *People,* "the music is okay with me—it's a genuine expression. You know kids are going to do exactly the opposite of what you think they ought to do." Most thought that Mel was lying when he critiqued his daughter's music, but everyone knew that he was telling the truth when he expressed the fact that she was going against his wishes by taking a wild and wide turn around country music.

Yet even as good as she was on stage and as happy as

she was to be in her own small spotlight, Pam longed for something more than just covering the top songs of the day. She would admit that while almost any kind of performing gave her a real charge, "What I really wanted to do was sing my own stuff."

With that in mind, even though she was now being recorded by a number of hot new acts in several different musical styles, she was in effect suiciding her songwriting career by saving her best stuff for herself. If she had had a record deal, this might have been a good idea, but to do so without one was considered pretty stupid by most in Music City. Besides, who was even going to consider recording a white female bluesy rocker in the middle of the Bible belt?

That was when famed Nashville producer and old friend Jimmy Bowen came back into the picture. As he and Pam got together to sort out different ideas and concepts, as well as discuss the singer's personal goals, Jimmy began to get Tillis to focus on developing a master plan. Up until this point, she had been all over the board. She had sung one style one night and another the next. There were few common threads in the music she wrote. She was simply never going to make it in the industry that she loved until she decided who she really was and what she really wanted to do with that person.

"We spent a lot of time talking about direction," Pam recalled as she looked back on the early meetings with Bowen. "He wanted to know where I wanted to go with my music. He was the one who really gave me a shot at doing what I wanted, what I knew I was best at." That, of course, was making it on the rock side of the charts.

Carving out a career as a pop or rock singer in Nashville was an uphill climb at best. L.A. was home to the rockers. That is where Tanya Tucker had gone when she had decided to try her best to become the female Elvis. In spite of millions of dollars in publicity, a searing album cover and sexy publicity pictures, and a host of high-profile club dates, the teenage superstar had fallen on her face. Yet, even while knowing the risks of alienating the city that had made her a star, Tucker had made the move and pushed full bore into rock music. She had "joined" the L.A. crowd.

Perhaps the fact that Pam said she wanted to cut rock music, to sing it on stage and in concert, but not to leave Tennessee showed that Pam was not as committed to this kind of musical expression as she wanted everyone to believe. L.A. and New York had the producers and the publicity machines. These were the places where the *Entertainment Tonight* cameras would find you and "give" you the high profile spots that could launch your career. Here is where the press that covered pop music wrote their copy and made their contacts. The coasts were the areas where it was happening.

Yet as firmly set on recording rock as Pam was, she was just as firmly set on staying home to do it. One of the main reasons had to be her son, Ben. She didn't want to leave him and she didn't want to take him to New York or Los Angeles. She simply didn't believe that the city was the place to raise a child. Maybe it was because she had often felt that her own father had put his family behind his career, Pam did just the opposite. She put Ben first.

Even as Pam prepared to go rock, her father hadn't given up on changing her mind. He often reminded her that she had sung backup on his huge 1980 country hit, "Your Body Is an Outlaw." The song wouldn't have been the same without her contributions and it made it to number three and stayed on the charts for four months. To Mel it seemed obvious that country music was where Pam's voice was most at home. So Mel warned her time and time again against deserting her roots. The elder Tillis was sure that Pam should stick with country. He argued that across the whole nation and much of the world the Tillis name means country. As she always had before, she rebelled. Pam even told her father, the man who could have gotten her a record contract with just a couple of short telephone calls, that she thought the songs he picked out for her were terrible.

A decade later, after she began to have success in country music, Pam looked back on this time period in an interview with *B.M.I.* By this point she had recognized just how much Mel had given her during this early phase of her career.

"Did my father influence me?" Pam had asked. She then answered herself, "Of course. I grew up in music watching him communicate with his audiences. Before I even knew what it really meant, I was saying that I wanted to be a singer. Being a performer is more difficult than I appreciated as a youngster, but it's worth it. You sort of get hooked and it's in your blood. Naturally, any son or daughter of a famous parent may have identity problems. You have to establish yourself as an individual. Sure, all the opportunities are there . . . sometimes before you are ready for them. The thing is to develop at your own pace. I do remember one bit of advice my father gave me. 'Remember, the most important thing in this business is survival.' He always encouraged me to write. 'Sing and perform,' he'd say, 'but never lose sight of writing and how important it is.' "

Pam certainly was writing, even though at that time Mel couldn't see how she was going to survive on the kind of stuff she was turning out. He also couldn't understand what she was doing with her voice. He saw her as a pure country vocalist, one of the best potential talents in Music City. But what Pam did when she opened her mouth was usually anything but country.

"Well, it's certainly my own hybrid vocal style," Pam told reporters at the time. Then painting a portrait that at least included a bit of her father's music, she added, "I like it all: rockabilly, honky-tonk, Celtic folk—and you can't go back further than that. Even on something that might be bluegrass, you're going to hear some soul licks and on some of the more progressive things, there's definitely some twang because it's all part of who and what I am."

Yet the more she got into rock and the blues, the less that twang carried through. And because people expected country music to be in her heart and because she was still living in Nashville, critics and fans were always watching to judge her, probably much too fast. In many cases she simply didn't get a chance to prove herself. A large percentage of the Nashville music community, almost everyone in power but Jimmy Bowen, felt as if Pam were turning her back on people who could help her have a much easier path to stardom. Even outside of Music City, when Pam took her act on the road, the critics tended to be harsh.

In 1982, she performed at the Sparks Nugget in Reno. *Variety* was there to catch Mel's daughter in action. In the next issue the reviewer commented on the young Tillis's show.

"Pam Tillis is to be commended for not automatically going country in her music. However, the direction she takes is wrong for her. She simply lacks the guts for New Wave and the other hard-edged sounds she tried. The roughness intended for the lyrics comes off sounding whiny. Tillis's better area is MOR [Middle of the Road].

"Tillis has little stage presence (her stage chat was almost exclusively 'We'd like to do a song right now . . . ') and her movements are awkward. Another problem is a weak band. There's a certain amount of curiosity about this show because of the name, and that translates to okay attendance figures; but word of mouth's not going to bring in much more business, and few are likely to return. Changing directions, naturally avoiding Daddy's territory for the most part, can help."

There were a number of *Variety* readers in Nashville who couldn't help but think, "I told you so." Some even believed that this might just teach the stubborn Tillis a lesson. They were tired of her "hell on wheels" music and the attitude that went with it. Pam's embracing of the styles of Linda Ronstadt; the Eagles; and Crosby, Stills, Nash, and

Young, instead of her father's sounds smacked of a child out of control, of a young woman who needed to be brought back down to earth. Some even thought that she was headed for a career crash that would make the automobile wreck of her teen years look like a fender bender.

Pam didn't have to be reminded of what a crash like that could do. She was still in great pain from having her face shattered in more than two dozen places. Yet many wondered if the pain of the accident would compare to the pain that Music City could inflict if Pam failed to follow what most thought of as the "proper career path." Tanya Tucker was now feeling that pain. She was being shunned. She had walked away from Nashville and the folks who had once embraced her now wouldn't even acknowledge her. At that time in country music, you could drink yourself into oblivion, miss bookings, beat your wife, marry and divorce, and spend time in jail, and still be pardoned by country music fans and radio. But if you left country music to try your wings in rock and roll, you were considered past help. It was like being a leper. No one wanted to touch you. This was probably what concerned Mel the most. He didn't want his flesh and blood to be shunned by the city and industry that had made him a star. And it certainly appeared that Pam was willingly headed in that direction.

Chapter Five

In one way Pam Tillis never left country music. There was a part of it that was always at least faintly visible in her work. Yet in another way she valiantly attempted to put it behind her when she jumped headfirst into the wide-open, high-speed world of rock music.

As Pam would tell the press when she looked back on her first seemingly serious run at the music industry in 1983, "I think I chose pop and rock and R&B, anything but country, because I didn't like competing with him [Mel] on his turf."

Certainly she would have been competing with her father if she had chosen country music at this time. In 1983 Mel may have been three or four years past his prime, but he was still hitting the charts for his new label MCA. "In the Middle of the Night" would even crack the top ten in the spring. Yet by and large, it wasn't really Mel with whom Pam was competing. It was his solid country image. When you observed the current crop of hot country acts—Ronnie Milsap, Eddie Rabbitt, and Barbara Mandrell—and then compared them to Mel Tillis, it was Mel who stood out as the "country bumpkin."

This Tillis "country bumpkin" image had to hurt Pam's chances to establish her own identity in Nashville. When the name Tillis came up, more often than not it conjured up images of jokes, not music. She was more than just a daughter of a famous country music singer/songwriter, she was the offspring of a comedian, too. Yes, the Tillis name stood for something, but what it stood for seemed so confining. And Pam hated to be confined almost as much as she hated labels. She felt that how people perceived her was somebody else's problem, and no one and nothing could or should limit her. She was her father's daughter, but she wanted people to know that she wasn't very much like him. On top of that, she didn't want to be. Yet as she tried to carve out her own career niche in Nashville, this attitude seemed to work against her. Many people even resented the fact that she didn't want to be like Daddy. They didn't want Mel's daughter to be a rebel.

In a very real sense, Pam simply couldn't escape what the Tillis name stood for at that time. Even as country began to be driven by the rock-influenced sounds of bands like Alabama and individuals such as Hank Williams, Jr., it seemed that she was going to be expected to sing songs that sounded like "I Ain't Never," her father's decade-old biggest hit. And when she didn't, many of those who came to see her simply because she was a Tillis left either unmoved, confused, or angry.

Now twenty-six, a single mother, and watching time slowly slip by, Pam was in a hurry to make a statement—her statement. It was time for her to finally step out and demand a spotlight. In spite of the fact that she knew that the cards were stacked against her, she chose to look for that spotlight in the world of rock music. How was her timing?

Most country acts who had tried this move had failed miserably. Rock music at the time also lacked focus. This fragmentation of the rock sound had paved the way for a horde of baby boomers to jump over to country music. Barbara Mandrell had even hosted a country music-inspired network television series that had given the then-struggling NBC television network a hit. Barbara was knocking pop stars like Barbra Streisand and Bette Midler out of the "People's Choice" awards. With lawyers in New York wearing boots, it looked as if country music was the happening place to be. Why, even a television show about a family in Dallas had the whole world abuzz. But was it a good place for someone like Pam? Was there room for her unique mix of jazz, rock, and soul in country?

In 1983, country music began the year by giving a redheaded Oklahoman her first number one. "Can't Even Get the Blues" was Reba McEntire's initial trip up to the top of the Billboard charts. With her musical twang and her pronounced accent, she was as country-sounding as any country music female star since Loretta Lynn. Her look at the time emphasized that image. She was a long way from what Pam Tillis wanted to be.

On the rock side, Daryl Hall and John Oates owned the year's first number one with "Maneater." At this point in time, Pam's stuff sounded a great deal more like Hall and Oates than Reba. So what choice did she really have? If she wanted to make a move right then, she probably had none. Nashville wasn't ready for her. K. T. Oslin and Steve Earle hadn't shown up yet to pave the way.

What it took to make Pam's move to rock official and complete was a record deal. Warner Brothers records signed her and brought in Jody Hill Productions and Dixie Gamble-Bowen (the Bowen connection finally paid off) to produce what they hoped would be an emerging singer/songwriter. Pam joked about the new project being funded by the folks who owned and produced "Looney Tunes." She even laughed about being paid in "bunny money." As would be proven over the next few months, the jokes were simply a foreshadowing of the project's future.

The 1983 LP *Above and Beyond the Doll of Cutey* was new wave music, a far cry from what was usually produced in Music City. Yet the strangely named album was cut in Nashville, as well as in Los Angeles, and there was a bit of the Tennessee influence in the package. Making sure that she was true to herself in almost everyway, every one of the cuts on the new release was at least cowritten by Pam. The other contributing writers were mainly folks she had gotten to know through the Nashville music scene. In the studio Warner brought in members of some of rock music's hottest bands to bring a true rock sound to Pam's original songs. Included in this rather unusual mix were members of the group who backed Kim Carnes, as well as the Motels, Jimmy Buffett, and the Eagles. Warner Brothers and Pam were hoping that some of the success that these musicians were experiencing would prove to be a golden touch for *Above and Beyond the Doll of Cutey.*

Kim Carnes had held number one for nine weeks just two years before with "Bette Davis Eyes." Certainly her band knew what it was like to hit the big time and produce hits. The Motels were at their peak period, having just scored with two top ten singles, "Only the Lonely" and "Suddenly Last Summer." Buffett's signature song, "Margaritaville," was already being considered a classic. Meanwhile, the Eagles were a decade into a career that had produced some of the greatest rock songs of the era. Included in these were "Lyin' Eyes," "Take It to the Limit," "Heartache Tonight," and "Hotel California." It was an all-star gathering, but the results would eventually hit the public as more of a "Merrie Melodies" staff party.

As if dreamed up by the folks who produced Bugs Bunny cartoons, the album's strange title seemed to mean very little. While it may have made no sense, it did serve to get people's immediate attention. With that in mind, the label's publicity machine began to pour out copy that extolled Pam, the album, and the new wave sound.

One studio press release proudly stated, "From the opening notes of *Above and Beyond the Doll of Cutey,* Pam Tillis's debut album for Warner Brothers, it's obvious that an unusual, and unusually talented, new artist is at work. This collection of ten original tunes defied expectations at every turn, turning convention on its ear and taking the listener on a fast-paced musical joy ride. Vocalist/songwriter Pam Tillis is nothing if not daring and *Above and Beyond the Doll of Cutey* is anything but predictable.''

Certainly she wasn't predictable, at least no more predictable than another Warner's star, Wile E. Coyote, and the folks in Nashville had known that for a long time. Yet how big a departure was this project from the singer's own country roots? One quick listen revealed that the album's lyrics had a cutting-edge razor-sharp country feel. Pam had a hand in writing every cut, and her work with some of Nashville's best in Mel's publishing company had obviously had an impact. Much more than in rock music, it was the lyric that mattered in country. Such was the case with the copy in *Above and Beyond the Doll of Cutey.* But the album itself was anything but the grass roots twang that might have commonly accompanied those Music City scored words. As the guitars and bass drove the action, Pam's first and last pop effort was straightforward rock and roll with a new wave feel. It was on the edge. As the Warner's press release boasted, ''both Pam Tillis and her music are among the freshest, most original and accessible new arrivals in quite a spell.''

Many in Nashville, where the album got very little play, expected the project to be panned. They felt that Warner had an ACME-style bomb on its hands. Yet rather than flunking the effort, *People* magazine gave it a B+. That was an exceptional mark for an initial release. In another review, *Stereo Review* chimed in with a C. Many of the best in the business would have loved to have earned such early praise. Certainly it was something that Pam and the label could look to with a great deal of hope. So there seemed to be no doubt the album proved that Pam was creative, but how would be it be accepted as it hit the stores? Would generally good reviews turn into good sales? Would people buy it and would radio stations play it?

As Pam hit the press run for the expected interviews, she trumpeted what she saw as the new release's best features.

The one thing that she emphasized again and again was, "It's an album that really reflects all the growth I've gone through since I started singing and writing. It's music that's me."

And the fact that this work truly represented the Pam of that time may have been one of the problems. It simply wasn't very well focused. In spite of the good reviews, the total package didn't have a theme or a consistent feel. In the past decade she had been all over the musical map. She had done punk, disco, soul, R&B, rock, country, and even jug music. She had immersed herself in jazz and free-form and even studied folk. She was a little bit of everything but not a lot of anything. Even those who had followed her since her high school days couldn't define her musical style. In 1992 Pam told California writer J. G. Wirt that the album was "Pop, some kind of R&B, some middle-of-the-road rock. Kim Carnesy kind of rock'n'roll. New wavy, kind of Bangley. It was a real grab bag." But it was also a bag few people wanted to grab!

The fact was that customers rarely spent good money on grab bags. Buyers were wary of anything they couldn't judge before they wrote the check. When folks studied this release, they had to wonder. She was just like them on one song, but someone totally different on nine of the others. Who was Mel's daughter? And in reality it always came back to that.

Of course the album's title was a real source of confusion too. It sounded like a bad skit from the old *Sonny and Cher Comedy Hour.*

Of the album Pam later said, "It was the worst album title ever."

The name was one of the problems that was easy to point to. Still, the biggest problem was that radio pretty much ignored it. Pam had been around the business long enough to know that it didn't make any difference if it was rock or country or good or bad; if the disc jockeys didn't push the songs, they simply weren't going to fly.

As she continued to pitch the product, Pam had to take a close look at herself and begin to admit to being somewhat of a chameleon. She now had to recognize that she was an artist in search of a style. And because she had refused to take Ben and move to the West Coast, because she had stayed in the center of the country music industry rather than rubbing elbows with the movers and shakers in rock and pop music, you have to wonder if even she felt that this musical move had any real potential. It just didn't seem like she was willing to pay the whole price for success. If that was the case, could she really believe that she was going to make it in the genre?

One fact had been consistent about Pam, she had always been inspired by good nightclub work. Live audiences and direct contact with people got her juices flowing. She previewed her album's best and gave it her best shot, not when talking about it to the press, but rather when singing her new material to the fans. She toured the fairs and clubs with a band of regulars in an old school bus. It really did look like something from "Looney Tunes," something that Wile E. would be driving. Something that ACME would have manufactured. It was a disaster waiting to happen.

When Mel caught her act, he shook his head and said, "her music is kinda punk to me, the way she has 'em dressed and everything." He also admitted that he hadn't bothered to listen to her album. When he found out that the old bus he had just made fun of to the press was hers, he blushed and shrugged his shoulders. While he offered that he was proud of his daughter, old Mel would have rather had her back home than on stage singing "that" kind of music.

Pam sang in a style that echoed the current crop of female rock talents such as Pat Benatar. Yet the style she was using didn't set her apart in that world. When most artists get their first record deal, they kind of know who they are. Pam was more like a little girl waiting to grow up. She was something different every day. In other words, she was really struggling to find and define who she was in the world of rock music.

Yet as the year dragged by, it was becoming more and more obvious that few were taking Pam seriously. Traveling part-time for small club dates, living in a home surrounded by Chinese artifacts, keeping her son as the center of her life, Pam was just not the definition of a rocker. And fans and the press picked up on this. Maybe Warner Brothers had too!

After the album was released and the Warner Brothers publicity machine began to back off, Pam traveled to England and absorbed a bit of the British musical scene. She wanted to focus on the sounds of the era. She wanted to go to school and learn how to make herself into a rock queen. Yet this pilgrimage didn't give her the pat and solid answers for which she had hoped. Instead of helping to push her quest for rock music, it actually influenced her move back into country.

The more rock acts she saw and heard, the more producers she met, the more she allowed herself to be immersed in the creative end of the London rock scene, the more she began to realize that she was more like her father than she had ever imagined. She would talk about this realization with the Country Music Association's *Close Up Magazine* eight years later.

"Country music is really in my blood. It was a part of me that has been denied for so long, and it seemed like the time to express that side of me. I felt lost in the pop music shuffle. And I had this great team here at Warner Brothers and no desire to relocate to a rock capital." She may have been a long way from Nashville, but she was seeing home and what it meant a lot more clearly than she ever had before.

As the slow sales continued and the experiment in new wave really began to fall apart, Pam seemed almost glad she had failed. She would tell her friends that "in rock she felt like she was pulling a chain." And that chain was keeping her from really being herself. In a very real sense, this experience had been a wake-up call for the young woman who had been running from the Tillis image.

She would tell the press at the time that she was not old-fashioned, but she was a Southern girl. And it was a Southern girl who had a great desire to come home from London to find herself. Back from England, she began to look seriously at what she might be able to contribute to the music that had defined Nashville. Mel might not have believed it then, but his daughter was beginning to settle down.

"From now on, I hope to be in all kinds of performance situations," Pam announced. "Especially so I can mix together my country and soul roots and other things that I've ignored for so long that are an integral part of me."

In country music, the year ended with Larry Gatlin and the Gatlin Brothers owning the charts with their "Houston (Means I'm One Day Closer to You)." It would be the last number one song for the brothers. Others who were experiencing a decline included Barbara Mandrell, T. G. Shepherd, and Janie Fricke. Among those bubbling under and ready to make a move up was a former Broadway chorus singer and folk artist, K. T. Oslin. On the rock side, former Beatle Paul McCartney and former Jackson Five sensation Michael Jackson were ruling the top spot with "Say, Say, Say." Jackson, who would have far more cosmetic surgery done over the next few years than Pam had had after the near fatal car crash, was the "King of Pop." It would have probably been hard for Pam to see herself singing a duet with Jackson. His world was certainly not hers. But maybe she could sing a duo with someone like Hank, Jr. They had something in common! Just looking at the close of the 1983 chart movement makes it easy to understand how Pam now seemed to feel a closer kinship to country music than rock. It was amazing to note what a difference a year could make.

Just like the coyote that had to chase the road runner even though he didn't really have the ammunition to bring him in, Pam's rock experiment was one that probably had to be made. She had to discover firsthand how different she was from the pop music scene. Fortunately, unlike Tanya Tucker who had burned her bridges when she had left to become the "female Elvis," Pam had continued to cling to her country roots and her country lifestyle. So there was a place for her to come home to.

Pam was now ready to see what the Tillis name could do for her in country music. It was time to put it all together and embrace who she really was. Unfortunately, it wouldn't happen overnight!

Chapter Six

In 1984, Pam finally decided to go the country music route for real. After her false start in rock, after discovering that her views of the music industry's direction and hers were a great deal different, after realizing even in that more liberal marketplace she really couldn't escape the precast image created by her last name, she generally embraced the fact that she was going to make it or break it in the same arena as her father had. Still, just as she hadn't given her whole heart to her rock effort by moving to Los Angeles and working the club scene there, many felt that she wasn't ready to give up on all her interest in other musical genres to concentrate on just country music.

But what else could she do? Deep down she must have realized that the rock music to which she had once felt so drawn was now heading a completely different direction. Many of those whom Pam had used as role models were now having problems landing hits on that side of the charts. Others had even come to Nashville in an attempt to begin anew with a fresh, positive, and simpler sound. No longer was rock music where it was happening. Besides, those who were making the big bucks over there fit more of the mold of Whitney Houston than Pam Tillis.

Things had changed enough in the music industry that Tanya Tucker had even come crawling back to Music City.

In spite of completely turning her back on country music in order to pursue the ''big time,'' Tucker was now begging folks in Nashville to give her another chance. She had all but admitted her mistaken rush to rock had been a disaster. Yet for Tucker, this return would take time. She had a lot of ''sins'' for which to atone, and the country music community would let her flounder for a while before welcoming her back into their arms.

Another who came back was Dolly Parton. Dolly had not made as dramatic a break as Tanya, but nevertheless, she had moved to Hollywood and attempted to create a sound that would ''rock'' the music world. Her pop music had sold better than Tucker's, but even the superstar Dolly hadn't charted on Billboard's rock side for three years. With her huge chest and giggling accent, more often than not in Hollywood she was considered a joke. In Nashville, Parton and her outlandish look may have labelled her as a joke, but at least in Tennessee she was a joke with talent. Yet Dolly and Tanya coming home was tame stuff compared to some of the others who were moving their music to Nashville at this time.

Leon Russell, a one-time member of Phil Spector's mighty ''Wall of Sound,'' and a rocker from way back, brought his unusual sound and style to Music City too. Russell had come in as a part of the ''Outlaw'' movement. He was one of the boys who Waylon and Wylie sang about in ''Luckenbach.'' Leon, who had once worked with Joe Cocker and had ridden the rock charts with anthems such as ''Tight Rope'' and ''Lady Blue,'' was now hitting the top in country with things like a remake of Elvis Presley's ''Heartbreak Hotel.'' If Music City had room for the pale, long-haired, eccentric Russell, maybe this once conservative community could make room for Mel's rebel daughter, too!

''I didn't get into country music until Leon Russell and Elvis Costello did some,'' Pam would tell the press when she radically changed her musical direction. Tillis would add, "Then I said, 'Wait a minute, I'm missing something here.' "

Truer words have never been spoken. Just like Tanya, what Pam was missing was the promise of any real money in rock music. For these two talented ladies, the youth-driven pop market was not an avenue which offered much in the way of career advancement. Yet now the music from which they had both run did seem to hold some potential. It was also true that the musical grass appeared a bit greener in Tennessee, and this resulted in a land rush of talent looking for gold.

During an interview with *Country Fever* in 1993, Pam looked back at the reasons she had decided to drop rock and jumped headfirst into the country scene. A great deal of it had to do with the fact she believed that Nashville was inclined at that time to be more accepting of a wider range of musical influences.

"In a nutshell," she told the magazine, "I started seeing that country music was changing. I once thought I couldn't be myself in country music. Country music was the music of my parents, but I saw it coming around more to the music I liked."

Pam also noted something else that was equally important to her thoughts that made it seem it was time for her to make her mark here in Music City. "There weren't many great women artists at that moment, and I decided that I had something to offer." This was something which Mel had been trying to show her for most of the decade.

As a matter of record, women artists in country music were there, but few seemed to be the real thing. The reigning queen, Barbara Mandrell, had been seriously injured in a car accident. At that time, some even doubted if she would ever be able to successfully tour full-time again. No one artist had risen to replace Mandrell. Janie Fricke, Sylvia, and Reba McEntire had won the last three Academy of Country Music's "Female Vocalist of the Year" awards, but two of these acts were mere lightweights on stage and

Reba was just learning how to wow a crowd. McEntire wasn't in Barbara's class yet. So there was room at the top, but just how large was this window of opportunity?

In all of 1983 and 1984, women artists had only held the number one spot on the Billboard country charts for fourteen weeks. And no woman had been able to maintain a top record for more than one week. It was a male-and group-dominated format. The door for female artists who had some degree of staying power was open, but the only person in the current crop who seemed to have the talent and the desire to work hard enough to take advantage of that was Reba. And even McEntire was a long way from proving herself in the big concert halls or at the cash register. Women were still considered by and large opening acts.

Even with the negatives, this atmosphere of change and open competition was enough to convince Pam to take a second look at the industry. The fact that more and more record labels were beginning to get heavily involved in country music worked to her benefit too! The explosion in country music probably meant that she was going to benefit, as were other female rock acts eyeing country like Juice Newton and Kim Carnes.

"I think when the new traditionalist thing started happening," she told *Country Fever,* "I got excited because, even though people might listen to my music and think it's really progressive, my country influences are '50s and '60s country music, the older stuff."

For most folks it seemed strange to hear Pam talking about her country roots. For years she had run away from them. Now she was actually claiming the sounds she had first heard when her father had brought some of the older artists over to their house after a show or recording gig or when she had been waiting backstage for her father at the Opry. Still, even though she liked what she was hearing and noted the growing opportunities for females in Music City, deep down she must have had some doubts. She still had to wonder if country music was big enough for two Tillises. This was something that Hank Williams, Jr. had contemplated for more than two decades until the genre had finally given him a real chance to make his kind of music in 1981. Would they do the same for her? Would country music be as accepting of her form of country mixed with rock as they were now with Hank's?

Pam later told *Tune-In,* "My feeling about letting go of this pop music dream sort of coincided with my songs and lyrics becoming more down-to-earth, and a lot more adult, and less able to fit on a pop play list."

Something else might have been a factor in her finally giving her all to country music. It was something that her father had recognized for years, something which she had rebelled against time and time again. Now she was admitting to herself, her record label, and even her dad, "I do this stuff [country music] good. I don't even have to learn it."

One of the first things Pam and Warner had to do was get ready to go back into the studio and lay down some country tracks. Another necessary move in this jump over to country was landing new management. Pam joined forces with Greil-Hooper Management and The Bobby Roberts Agency. Roberts had a solid reputation and still works with many of Nashville's top acts. These folks knew how to exploit Tillis's country roots while maximizing her individual sound and personality. They set to work doing just that.

Any good public relations firm knows that exposure is the primary factor in creating customer awareness. At that time in country music, the best place to gain exposure was via The Nashville Network.

TNN had been launched in March 1983 and had immediately become one of television's great success stories. One of broadcasting's giants, Gaylord Entertainment Company, sensed a need to fill the country music television void. Responding to the success of *Barbara Man-*

drell and the Mandrell Sisters's long run on NBC, as well as the tremendous ratings of the CMA awards show, the company jumped in with both feet to cable. One of the main reasons that TNN hit so strong so fast was a well-known country music disc jockey named Ralph Emery.

Ralph had seemingly been training for this opportunity for most of his life. Beginning at a small-town radio outlet, Emery had worked his way up the ladder to Nashville's WSM. There, as the home station of the "Grand Ole Opry," he found a home as an all-night DJ. Much of his show's charm was that country music stars came by to visit and plug their albums in a very informal atmosphere. He spun this success over to both syndicated radio and television, so Emery was more than primed and ready when TNN began looking for a host for the cable station's first ninety-minute nightly live variety show. Put together in a fashion that was half *Ed Sullivan* and half *The Tonight Show,* country music fans across the United States and Canada quickly became addicted to this window to live country music. The biggest names in the business turned out, and a host of up-and-comers wanted desperately to get on. One of these was Pam Tillis. She didn't have to wait long for her shot.

The audience that caught Pam on *Nashville Now,* the name given to Ralph's show, would have known nothing about her unsuccessful rock efforts. This would therefore offer the "new" country singer a chance to begin again. And second chances in this business were very rare indeed. Pam and her management team knew that her appearances with Ralph could be worth millions. If the fans fell in love with her on TNN, they would call radio stations and demand that her music be played when Warner finally had some country tracks ready for shipment.

Her initial appearance on "Nashville Now" came in 1984. Predictably, she was introduced to the large live crowd and the millions watching across the country as

"Mel Tillis's daughter." Surprisingly, she didn't sing a song she had written. Rather, for her debut, she chose a number that her dad had written for Brenda Lee. Pam had probably heard "Emotions" at her own home, and she had probably become even more familiar with it when she stayed with Brenda's mother. Miss Lee had taken it up the rock charts in 1960. The old Lee/Mel Tillis effort turned out to be a perfect choice for a crowd that had grown up listening to rock and roll during that time. And essentially, much of the TNN audience had done just that. The fact that Pam was still pushing a bit of a rock/blues sound made this song a natural choice too. And even as she sat on the couch with Ray Price and talked about her love of country music, Pam still didn't seem ready to give up on her natural love of rock and blues.

With her hair permed, Pam appeared thin and almost demure, but from her first hello, she allowed a hint of her sense of humor to peek through. As the show continued and Tillis responded to Ralph's questions, she seemed a bit shy. Her soft Southern voice sounded more sweet than confident. Yet she had no problem coming up with quick replies for questions which centered more on her father than herself. She explained that there were five Tillis children, and that proved that "he [Mel] did get home once in a while." She also informed the world that her father called her "Pamie Wong" because she had an oriental look, some of which had been created during her many facial surgeries. With tidbits like this, how could the audience not like her? But were they really getting to know the real Pam? Was Ralph and his line of questioning allowing Ms. Tillis to really shine through?

In reality, that initial appearance on *Nashville Now* had given young Pam a chance to reveal very little of herself to the country music fans, and what little they had learned probably wouldn't do her career much good. After one television appearance, a time when each sentence could mean something at the cash register, no one really knew who Pam was.

As her management team and label began to look at the tape of *Now* and Pam's concerts, they saw her greatest strength as her largest and most dangerous flaw. Her versatility, Tillis's ability to sing so many different styles so well, was once again not giving her a clear direction or identity. No matter the venue, Pam always seemed to want to mix country and soul. It had been done successfully before by the likes of Barbara Mandrell, and newcomer K. T. Oslin was attempting it now, but it was a tough sell. In many people's minds, it was like mixing water and oil. It would have been much simpler if Pam had simply stuck to straight country, but anyone who knew her also knew that she wasn't going to do that.

Warner's publicity machine, which just a few months before had been asking the public to forget about Pam's country background and judge her on her new rock sound, was now writing, "Say hello to the great country sound we have come to associate with the Tillis name." The company thought they had even wrangled her a chance to sing the title tune to the Hollywood western cowboy send off, "Rustler's Rhapsody." Unfortunately, Gary Morris landed that gig. That loss ultimately didn't matter too much since the movie bombed at the box office. In the meantime, as the movie faded, Pam's voice was being heard. She was cutting some pretty successful jingles for companies such as Hardees and Equal, the sugar-substitute. But this was not the kind of hit she really needed.

She began working with Barry Beckett, who had produced acts such as Aretha Franklin and Bob Dylan, as well as more recently Shelly West. With him, Pam was trying to find the right combination at Warner Brothers. At first they tried a very Muscle Shoals sound.

Muscle Shoals, which had long had some influence in country music, was hot. A real country band, the first since Bob Wills's Texas Playboys, had used this sound to climb the charts. Alabama was making more than just music—the four guys were selling records. Turning long-held expectations of country music record and concert sales upside down, this group was not just rocking country stations with a new sound, but bringing teenagers and college students by the hundreds of thousands into country music. Sales were in the millions and number-one records were the norm. In their first four years for RCA, Alabama would record twenty straight number-one records. Maybe not since Hank Williams had country music been shaken up so much by one act.

Suddenly across the nation, record scouts were out trying to find the next country band. Even former rock groups like Exile traveled to Nashville, tweaked their old styles a bit, and landed contracts and gigs. Promoters were even putting together a host of new manufactured groups based on the Alabama success formula. One of these, Atlanta, actually scored for a while. And why was all this action taking place? Because high schoolers in places like New York were buying pick-up trucks and wearing boots. This new demographic pattern had meant that country music was selling better than ever and selling in places that in the past hadn't even carried it. At the sold-out Alabama concerts, fans were acting like rock crowds and spending money like water. With all this in mind, Pam would have been stupid not to have tried to use this Muscle Shoals sound to expand into this new audience of country music fans.

But, by and large, it was the bands, not the female acts that were turning on the teens and rock converts to most things Nashville. These new fans weren't as of yet into the female acts. So Pam and her producers were forced to go back to the drawing boards searching for the right style of country music for her. While continuing to write on her own, Pam also turned the town upside-down trying to find songs to help her accomplish this mission.

"I have not single-mindedly pursued any direction of

music until recently,'' she admitted. ''I dabbled in rock and roll, which is a natural thing to go into when you are a teenager. Then I found I had a real knack for R&B, so I dabbled in that. The last couple of years, I got more serious about doing country things. I feel like I've been more focused the last couple of years.'' But where would that focus lead her, and could she turn her own music or the music she discovered in Nashville's best studios into a hit record?

As she listened to countless demos, she began to note the work of certain songwriters. One of these was a sometime performer, Bob DiPiero.

Pam told CMA's *Close Up's* Teresa George in 1991, ''And they kept playing me all of these songs I liked so much. And I'd go, 'Who wrote that one?' and they'd go, 'Bob DiPiero.' '' She liked what Bob had written so much that she finally tracked him down and met him.

DiPiero was a good person to know. Some of his things had already become hits, and many others soon would. The Oak Ridge Boys had recently taken Bob's ''American Made'' to the top of the charts. As she listened to his work, Pam noted that DiPiero had a host of other great songs, which—though Pam didn't feel they were right for her at the time—seemed as if they could be hits, too. His writing and his technique were strong, and what he was turning out seemed especially right for the times. With her own obvious talents and his administration of his talents, it probably wasn't surprising that when they met, there was an instant attraction—after all, they had so many things in common. Though Bob was married, the two songwriters quickly became good friends.

In Nashville, when songwriters become friends, they usually begin to share ideas. This sharing of concepts often leads to writing together. That was exactly the route that Bob and Pam followed and it led to Warner finding a single the duo had composed that the label felt Pam just might be able to sell to both radio and fans.

In late 1984, after more than a decade in the business, Warner Brothers released Pam's first real country single. "Goodbye Highway" had a country rock feel to it. It also had a new RCA artist who showed a great deal of talent helping Pam out. Adding vocal and guitar on "Highway" was Vince Gill.

A reviewer for the *Vegas Visitor* wrote of the release, "A heartfelt example of her [Pam's] abiding love and instinctive feel for country music. In her music, she shows the kind of unerring talent millions have long enjoyed in her famous father. [She has] a voice for a whole new generation of country-music lovers."

In spite of those glowing words, music lovers largely ignored Pam and the single. This was all the more shocking to the label because of the fact that the song's lyrics had been inspired by Pam's own life. Usually personal stories worked so well on records. So, in spite of the solid production work and great country music sound in the single, "Lost Highway" was just that, lost. It lasted five brief weeks on the charts, topping out at number seventy-one, before fading fast.

On a second appearance on *Nashville Now* in early 1985, Pam pushed her first Warner's release. This effort came in spite of the fact that the song had already been pushed from radio station playlists. Ralph's country audience seemed to really appreciate Pam's rousing live version of "Goodbye Highway." Yet what they obviously appreciated even more was that Pam would be sitting on the couch sharing time with *Now*'s other guest. The headline star that night was Mel.

Right off the bat, Mel told Emery, "I think she's good [performer] and she's a good writer, too." Yet as he talked, he seemed much more proud of the grandson Ben than what Pam had given him through her music. When Pam did get the chance to talk on her own, she seemed to be a bit more confident and seemed more like a seasoned entertainer than she had been during her first appearance on the cable show. Ironically, one of the biggest reactions she got from the crowd and the host was when she admitted that she hadn't read her father's autobiography. After watching the humorous reaction to this, Pam then let it slip that it was her mom, Mel's ex-wife, not her father who named her.

As the interview progressed, Emery got Pam to admit that it seemed that she had been "struggling to get out of the shadows forever. People remember your name, but it's what you do on the other side of the door that matters." For a change, Ralph had gotten beneath the surface and hit on a real point that revealed a bit of Pam's frustration with country music.

Then, in a follow-up question that seemed a bit ill-timed, Ralph missed his chance to dig more deeply into the emotion and heartache of not being recognized on her own merits. Emery seemed to also blunder when he inquired about the chance of Pam stepping right back into the shadows and doing a duet with her father. She shrugged her shoulders and answered that if the right one came along she might, but then she added assertively, "I'm trying to stand on my own first." Shaking his head, the host attempted to encourage Pam by pointing to the success of Hank Williams, Jr. and Crystal Gayle. Mel quickly added, "Cream rises to the top. When she finds what she does best, it will happen."

As that edition of *Nashville Now* concluded, it appeared that Mel was much more in touch with what Pam needed to jumpstart her career than was Ralph Emery. The elder Tillis sensed that a duet with a fading star like himself would mean little for his daughter's career, what she really needed was a song and a sound that would give her career some identity. Right now she was still stumbling along in the dark. Mel had always known what kind of music he wanted to do, but his daughter didn't seem to have a set goal! Until she got one, she wouldn't be a success.

Warner's opted to release a ballad for Pam's second single. "It's Just One of Those Things," penned by Pam, Mary Ann Kennedy, and Pam Rose, never charted at all. One reviewer stated of the release, "Its sound is clean, undiluted country and Pam's voice, never sounding better, is enhanced by the skillful guitar and back-up vocals of Vince Gill." The good words mattered not at all; the song crashed just after take-off.

Working small-town dates and watching records die was not a great deal of fun, nor did it signal much hope for the future. Pam's record label was getting edgy, and in truth so was she. Finally a bit of good news came along in 1985 when Pam was signed to write for Tree and BMI. Here, at one of Nashville's best publishing houses, she got to work on a regular basis with three of Music City's most promising writers: Bob DiPiero, Gary Nicholson, and Rick Carnes.

Pam had always used songwriting as a way to understand herself. Even back when she was a child, it had helped her define her feelings and emotions. In the midst of a recording career that was stuck in the mud, and at a dismal point in her jump into country music, writing with creative force was a positive outlet. This was a way to regain her confidence and her voice.

While Pam was creating lyrics and music, country music was beginning to make waves of its own. Some of the best and most respected magazines in the nation were noting the success of The Nashville Network and the growth of country music while trying to figure out what was driving this move. In August 1985, *Newsweek* ordered a feature piece called "Nashville's New Class." The story was built around the crop of new female talent who were putting their marks on country music.

This outlet would have been a great place for Pam Tillis to have earned some much-needed exposure. *Newsweek* could have worked some magic if the periodical had devoted at least a portion of their story to Mel's daughter. But much of the interview centered on folks like Kathy

Mattea, Gail Davies, and Roseanne Cash. When the magazine finished with those three, the Judds were highlighted as an up-and-coming duo. The magazines seemed to pick these women because the writers felt they had the best chance to join Reba McEntire as those vying to replace an ailing Barbara Mandrell as country music's next queen. As time would show, their choice of Reba was correct, but they missed badly on Davies and Mattea. And while Cash was hot for a time, even this talent soon became lost in McEntire's growing shadow. Hence, the red-head became the story's main focus. When Pam was included, she was used simply to comment on Reba. Tillis's quote, though honest and straightforward, also got her into hot water. Pam told *Newsweek,* "Reba's *happenin'*. I like her whole trip. She's pure. I love somebody with that sort of stiff-ass vision. She's got a cause."

In looking truthfully and expressively at Reba's career, Pam probably also realized just what was wrong with her own. She didn't have a vision. She didn't have a real cause. She couldn't put her finger on her own goals. Worst of all, her father had been telling her this for years.

"Those Memories of You," a hard country song, was shipped as Pam's third single for Warner's country division. It hit the charts during the first month of 1986. This song, her biggest "hit" for the label, would peak at number 55 and remain on the playlist for eight weeks. The release was very country and more traditional sounding than Pam's usual musical vehicles. Even though it made few waves on country music radio, it was really good material. So good in fact that Dolly Parton, Emmylou Harris, and Linda Ronstadt recut the song a year later and rode it into the chart's top ten. A ride like this would have made Pam's career. For Dolly it simply signaled that she was now really back at the center of the Nashville music scene. Parton made the point that *Newsweek* should have spent a bit more time and a wide-angle focus on a certain big busted blonde, too!

As Pam and Warner continued to search for the right formula, Tillis continued to work the one venue that offered her some solid exposure, TNN. Over the course of the next year, Pam hit *Nashville Now* at least a half a dozen more times. She now wore lots of lace and satin and sat next to folks like Ronnie McDowell and Roy Acuff. She also was forced to answer many of the same questions about her father that she had been answering for years. Ralph Emery, as well as his guest hosts, wanted to know more about the funny times with Mel than they did about the good things going on in Pam's own career. In the face of this "typecasting" as a star's child novelty act, Pam more often than not exhibited a great deal of patience and a growing confidence in herself. Not once did she show her frustration in this overused line of questioning.

Another problem was that it seemed that after every song she sang on *Now*, Ralph complimented her on the fact that she sang so well, and felt a need to inform the audience that she was a local favorite. This alone should have counted for something, but the host almost always followed his compliments with the question, "Have you got a record deal yet?" The fact that she had had a label for two years, had released a handful of singles, and had talked about Warner, her records and her enthusiasm about them each time she had been on the show seemed lost on the host. It was like he wasn't paying attention to her or taking her seriously. And if Ralph Emery couldn't remember that Pam was a recording artist, then how could the people who bought country music records or called into radio stations with requests?

One of Emery's most interesting questions to Pam came during her final days as a Warner act. Ralph asked, "Have you been discovered yet?"

Pam answered the question hopefully by talking about the "good buzz" on the radio, and that she was looking forward to making it big because "then people don't care what you do." As it then became obvious that Ralph couldn't quite figure out just what it was that Pam was doing or where it was she was heading in country music, Pam joked that she was using the "Zen approach to show business. This leaves room for creativity."

Warner, which now seemed to have hundreds of Pam Tillis tracks, began to wonder if they might just be tossing bad "bunny money" after more bad "bunny money." After "Those Memories of You," "I Thought I'd About Had It with You" spent four weeks on the charts and peaked at number 67. Then "I Wish She Wouldn't Treat You That Way" rose to only number 69. Tillis's last single try for Warner struggled mightily to make it to number 71 on its six-week journey on the country music playlist.

During this period, it must have seemed that every eye in Nashville was on Pam, watching to see when she was going to be "discovered." Everybody, including those who still believed in her, seemed to be saying, "Pam, hurry up." Yet, nothing could push along her transition into country any faster than it was happening. She would have loved to hurry up, she just didn't know how!

In 1986, Pam played the "Big E," the New England Exposition, in Springfield, Massachusetts, doing three shows a day while showing off her Warners wares. Her stage outfits had gotten wilder, animal print pants and lots of lace, and she was making an impact with her humor. She jokingly referred to herself as the "good daughter gone bad." Yet as good as the shows were, the career prospects weren't improving. More folks walked by than stopped in. Now it seemed that most folks weren't even curious about the Tillis name.

In September, she returned to *Nashville Now* and asked the musical question "What Would Elvis Do?" Pam had written the song with Rick Carnes and it was obvious through her performance that she loved it. Marshall Morgan, who was now producing her, agreed that this song was creative and entertaining. But it wasn't released, and there was nothing that even Elvis could do to jumpstart young

Tillis's Warners stock. Wile E. Coyote probably should have been her mascot.

Pam, who was by this time often introduced as Music City's top underrated talent, sponsored a hoedown billed as "Twang Night" at Twelfth and Porter in Nashville. Joining her on the bill was Rick and Janis Carnes, Bill Lloyd, Kathy Chiavola, Leroy Preston, and Becky Hinson. The crowd who came loved her and her performer friends, but while informal shows like this were fun, they weren't putting her on the charts. They weren't brightening her dimming spotlight.

A big break looked like it was in the cards when Pam was invited to showcase her talents at a famed local club, the Nashville Palace. In a review of one of the first shows in her week-long engagement, Michael McCall of the *Nashville Banner* noted, "Unlike her famous father, Pam Tillis does not stutter. Nor does she sing traditional country music. But she does sing and her squeaky-doll voice can turn inside out with gutty emotion when she pops into her best songs.

"Though a country heart lies underneath, the surface of her songs includes a youthful rock energy and more than a little bit of soul. So expect a drumbeat and some truth."

When he caught her act, noted writer Robert K. Oermann wrote that "Versatile" is her middle name. "In all of the styles she has tried, she's been astoundingly good. Her torrid voice, so full of riveting tension, is the envy of almost every female singer in Music City."

Yet while some of Nashville's most important critics loved Pam, and some of country music's best-known female vocalists were big fans, it was doing nothing for her career. Even when she worked the famed strip at the Landmark in Vegas, it turned out to be another false start.

When she had left rock, Pam had somehow felt that country music was ready for her and her eclectic style. Almost three years after making the move, it appeared that Music City was no more ready for her than folks who bought rock and new wave had been. Even in an arena that had offered her national television exposure countless times and dates in some of country music's best clubs, she had not taken off. It was now more than obvious that Warner was going to give up on her and turn their attention to other acts. With country and rock's doors now closing on her, where would Pam go?

Chapter Seven

"A lot of people will probably assume that I am handed everything," Pam Tillis explained as she sensed her career opportunities dwindling down to almost nothing. She then resolutely added, "You know, I am out there fighting it out with everybody else. It just hasn't been handed to me in any way, form, or fashion. I pay my rent and take care of my son. I do the whole thing."

When Pam Tillis began 1987, she had been in the music business on a more or less full-time basis for more than a decade, yet she was still laboring under the shadow of her father. This fact was compounded by the realization that by that time Mel was having no more recording success than Pam. While her days at Warner Brothers were fast winding down, Mr. Tillis was in the midst of working for three different labels—RCA, Mercury, and Radio—in the span of two years. The highest spot any of his records had hit on the charts was number 31 with "You'll Come Back, You Always Do." In the face of the tremendous success of the new groups such as Alabama, and the new male vocalists such as Ricky Van Shelton, Mel was often considered a "has-been." Whether he would have admitted it or not, the elder Tillis was finding that Music City offered him no more opportunities than it had recently given his daughter. With that fact in mind, the former CMA "Entertainer of the Year'' packed his bags and moved lock, stock, and barrel to Branson, Missouri. By opening his own theater there, Mel was hoping to cash in on the Ozarks the same way that Roy Clark had done a few years before.

Mel had always had a great sense of timing. For a stutterer, this was quite an accomplishment. He had made the move from songwriting to singing just when his style of music would appear fresh and honest. His move to the Ozarks came at the perfect moment too. His corny humor and superb showmanship would not just be valued here, but welcomed with open arms.

While Mel was quickly counting the dollars generated by his own ticket sales and proving that he always landed on his feet, Pam was laboring just to pay the bills. Not only was there no promise of success right around the corner, she couldn't even find a corner. Every road she had taken in recent days had turned into a dead end.

Still, with her father out of town, Pam probably should have felt a bit of relief. Logic would dictate that now she just might have the opportunity to do a few interviews without having most of the questions center on Mel. Yet even though he was out of sight, he was never out of the writers' minds. There were times in interviews when she must have wanted to scream. How many times could she answer ''What was the best thing you learned about the business from your dad?'' or ''What was the funniest thing you ever saw Mel do?'' or ''What is your favorite Mel Tillis song?'' While the questions were old and unoriginal, in some ways it was hard to fault the writers. Pam wasn't doing a great deal that could have generated a solid dialogue.

Warner released two Pam Tillis singles in 1987. While both charted, neither would come even close to being a hit. In order to help push a recording career that was running on just a couple of cylinders, Pam was still working the usual dates that most new talents were forced to work when they were building a serious recording career. In the middle of fairs and clubs, she also found time to get together in an almost informal manner with many of her Music City friends at local night spots as well. Here is one of the areas where she was most free to experiment with any sound, as well as test the waters for her latest compositions. When you work so hard, these moments of freedom are few and far between!

Her writing partner and friend Bob DiPiero had gotten a divorce from his wife and over time, Pam and Bob expanded their relationship. They began to see each other socially. At about the same time that the duo started dating, Bob was getting together with a few friends in a studio and trying to make a bit of musical magic of his own.

During the late seventies, one of the most popular Nashville club bands to emerge was Wolves in Cheap Clothing. Off and on throughout the eighties this band, consisting of John Scott Sherrill, Dennis Robbins, Martin Parker, Reno King, and Bob DiPiero, entertained at scores of club dates each year to enthusiastic crowds. The group's most talented members were probably Sherrill, Robbins, and DiPiero, all staff writers at Tree. Writing sometimes as individuals and sometimes in a team, the trio had turned out such hits as Highway 101's "(Do You Love Me) Just Say Yes," and "Cry, Cry, Cry," John Anderson's "Wild and Blue," Reba McEntire's "Little Rock," and Steve Earle's "Nowhere Road." Pam recognized talent and liked to be around creative folks who could help her grow. It was no wonder that Pam Tillis had been drawn to them, and in particular DiPiero. It was also no wonder that record labels were starting to show some interest in their group.

Sensing that Wolves in Cheap Clothing needed a few demo tracks of their own, Bob set about getting the guys together and recording the band at his own home on a 12-track system. Wanting to find a new handle to go with their tighter sound, the five guys reversed the term "Hillbilly," and changed it to Billy Hill. They then invented an individual, whose photo appeared with the false bio they had written, as this mysterious but talented country musician from deep in the hills of Tennessee. In time, the legend of Billy Hill grew and the group would land Billy a record deal at Reprise, the same label which had once given the world the music of Herb Albert, Dean Martin, and Nancy Sinatra.

Pam reacted to all this craziness in a completely positive way. She would have loved to have been a part of something this unique. And wouldn't it have been a great way for her to escape her father's shadow! To create a character from scratch! To invent parents and historical data, and then wear a disguise on stage. Yet for now this dream was impossible, and all she could do was watch the guys perform and work with them as they wrote.

During this period of time, when her career was all but flat, with the records going nowhere and her live dates not even paying the bills, Tillis was extremely glad that she had taken Tree Publishing's Paul Worley up on his offer to be a staff writer. As she explained to friends, "It meant I wouldn't have to go knocking on doors, crawling on my hands and knees." But there was more to her wanting a job at this hallowed house than just getting a writer's draw. She admitted as much when she said, "But I guess you could say I had an ulterior motive [for taking the job] too. I knew Paul's production work, and he was saying maybe we could also do some kind of production deal on the side. He'd put some tapes together on me."

As her friends knew and Paul Worley was soon to find out, knowing that it was all but over at Warner hadn't caused Pam to give up on her performing career. She still believed that she had potential, she just hadn't found the right people to bring it out yet. When she did, she knew that she could sell records. In the meantime, she also realized that the best way to impress Music City with her own talents was to follow the same route her father had used when he was building his career, through songwriting. Being on staff at Tree was one thing, but writing hits was another. Through inspiration, sweat, and hard work, Pam

The Forester Sisters were hot and Pam Tillis was on her way up when this was taken in 1985. *(Photo © Vicki Houston)*

Mel Tillis with his second wife at the Country Music Hall Of Fame in 1985. *(Photo © Vicki Houston)*

Two of Arista's biggest acts, Michelle Wright and Pam Tillis, in 1990. *(Photo © Vicki Houston)*

Pam's husband, Bob DiPiero *(left)*, shown with Randy Owen of Alabama, and Country DJ Gerry House in 1994. *(Photo © Vicki Houston)*

Taken just before going on stage in a Nashville 1996 show, Pam is confident, friendly and always ready to take another moment for a question, a request or a photo. *(Photo © Vicki Houston)*

Pam Tillis in Nashville at Fan Fair in 1996. Another day of putting on a show for more than 25,000 people. *(Photo © Vicki Houston)*

Pam Tillis in Nashville at her Fan Fair Booth in 1996. Pam takes her fans' wishes for her time very seriously. *(Photo © Vicki Houston)*

It's another hit, this one during a charity softball game in 1997. *(Photo © Vicki Houston)*

Pam wowing an overflow crowd in Nashville in 1997. *(Photo © Vicki Houston)*

An entertainer who cares as much about giving herself to her fans, Pam is also a songwriter who is not afraid to bare her life story in her work. *(Photo © Vicki Houston)*

soon became heavily involved in doing the latter. She was being recorded by the likes of Suzy Boggus, a new Capital artist, and Wild Rose, a new female band, then with Universal. Rock folks such as Cee Cee Chapman and Earth Day Project, as well as country music vets, Janie Fricke, The Forester Sisters, Highway 101, Juice Newton, Judy Rodman, Conway Twitty, and Ricky Van Shelton were covering her originals as well. Willie Nelson, had once said that you write your best stuff when you're hungry. If this is the case, then Pam must have been really hungry because she was writing better than she ever had. Yet in some ways, the same thing which was bringing her much-needed success and earning her an industry-wide name as a songwriter, was also getting in the way of her personal life.

Pam Tillis was extremely energetic. She always had been. When she wasn't writing, performing, or being a full-time mom, she was involved in such things as reading the latest hit books, going to movies, collecting antiques, cooking, painting, and sewing. There was no place where she didn't try her creative wings. She was constantly endeavoring to expand her mind and her opportunities. Yet as she and Bob DiPiero began to date more, she feared that their relationship would close a door that she felt was far too important to shut. She didn't want to strain her songwriting opportunities with Bob or any of his friends. If they committed to a relationship, Pam was sure that the writing would suffer. Right now, her career was simply more important than personal feelings. She essentially wrote a "Dear John" ending to their budding romance.

This line in the sand which Pam drew might have signalled that she was finally ready to jump into the business with both feet. To do what her father had done during his rise—put her personal life on the back burner. She was ready to really make some sacrifices. In the past she had limited her actions and efforts by not moving to Los Angeles and getting heavily involved in the rock music world, or not really pushing the straight country ties when Warner had marketed her that way. She had always held back a little. Now if she was even willing to break off a promising relationship because it might get in the way of her music, maybe she was really committed to her work. Industry-wide, folks were watching to see. The good things going on in the writing sessions were only a part of the formula for commercial success. Pam was also going to have to set off some fireworks in her live shows so that fans and disc jockeys would get excited enough to want to give her records a chance.

During the year, Pam opened several times for Larry Collins. Collins had been a part of country music since his eighth birthday. In the mid-fifties, Larry and his older sister Lorrie were child stars on a West Coast-based country music television show *Town Hall Party.* This was the same show that would later showcase a twelve-year-old Barbara Mandrell for the first time. Working with a rockabilly sound, the siblings had several minor hits toward the end of the decade. Though he continued to work as a country guitar player, Larry didn't emerge as a serious adult country act until he was given a cowriter's credit on the cross-over hit "Delta Dawn." He had followed that strong effort with "You're the Reason God Made Oklahoma." Still he had never approached the fame he had known as a child, and when he joined with Pam, Larry was on the last go-around of trying to make it back into the country music's main spotlight.

Tillis and Collins's best booking had come when the pair worked Billy Mo's in Vegas. The date was tied to both of them having earned Academy of Country Music nominations as best new acts. As it turned out, neither would win the award. K. T. Oslin grabbed the female honors, and Ricky Van Shelton ran away with the men's. After the ACM show, while Pam continued to ply her trade on the road, Larry soon sensed the gig was over. He gave up the guitar and became a golf pro. Ironically, when Collins walked away, his career looked no less promising than

Pam's. Of course, that wasn't saying much since no one was begging Larry to give it just one more try.

At the same time as a star as hot as Reba made plans to cut Pam's "Don't Rush Me, I'm Almost Gone," Pam was opening for the likes of Union Station, instead of the big acts like Clint Black. She had been all but forgotten by most fans, as well as the major labels, and "Don't Rush Me, I'm Almost Gone," could have been her personal motto. Many fully expected Pam to give up performing and stick to her writing.

One of the most ironic things about Pam's failure at Warner Brothers was not that her released songs didn't make a good showing when they landed on the charts, but rather the quality of the ones she cut which never got a chance to hit the playlists. Tillis was the first one to lay down the tracks for "Five Minutes." This song had hit written all over it. This was proven when another second-generation country star, Lorrie Morgan, released it in 1990. "Five Minutes" became Morgan's first number one single. Tillis's version didn't even get the time of day.

Pam also cut a version of "One of These Things," during her tenure at Warner. This tune would race up the charts in 1991 and top out at number six. It seems incredible that someone at Warner Brothers had not noted this one. After all, it would be Pam who took this same song into the top ten when she landed a gig at Arista. The first version couldn't even find the way to the playlist, while the second was a major hit.

Then, who would have believed that Pam found and recorded what was to become her signature song, "Maybe It Was Memphis," while at Warner Brothers. Like her other potentially great cuts, it simply disappeared. That first "Memphis" entered the Twilight Zone. It became another of "the lost hits of Pam Tillis." So it wasn't as if Warner didn't have the material, they just didn't seem to know what to do with it. This fact, not lost on Pam at the time, may have hurt her more than any other.

When Pam wasn't on the road, she continued to make appearances on Ralph Emery's *Nashville Now.* Like Lorrie Morgan, she appeared so many times on this TNN show that many people believed that at least one of the two country music offspring were there every night. Yet while this exposure seemed to be doing something special for Lorrie's career, it was not accomplishing much of anything for Pam. Was Lorrie more talented that Pam? No! But viewers did find Morgan more of a sex symbol, while Pam was just the girl next door. Maybe this was the reason Tillis's career didn't benefit from the exposure while Morgan's did.

One evening she told Ralph, "I am just waiting for all those things to eventually work together." Yet even as she said that, it appeared that everything was falling apart.

Music City News wrote in April 1987, "Pam Tillis has taken a 'circuitous route' in her musical career. She has been performing for the past ten years and is just now finding her place in country music."

Yet even as the "Bible" of country music was writing those encouraging words, Warner Brothers was giving up on the singer. The label had determined that Pam really didn't have a place in Music City's music scene. For all practical purposes, it now appeared that the only way Pam would ever get a chance to really make it in country music was through divine intervention.

Even though many were considering Pam a washed-up star who simply was never going to go anywhere in the business, Ms. Tillis was still heavily involved in making the best of her next potential chance. She had employed Renee Grant Williams as her voice coach and was working with the Nashville veteran to improve the quality and strength of her singing. In the process of visiting with Ms. Williams at a rehearsal, Pam began to talk about a touring Broadway musical which she had heard was coming to Nashville. Both women were looking forward to the opportunity to see Music City's version of *Jesus Christ Superstar.*

In truth, 1987 had been a pretty forgettable year in Pam's life, but for some reason, even though every sign signalled more of the same, she had a feeling that 1988 offered something better. As she travelled to Chicago and Los Angeles to cut jingles for commercials, she couldn't have begun to guess that this "better" opportunity involved a chance to sing and act in the musical she so badly wanted to see.

The news that Pam had shared with Renee had been accurate. *Jesus Christ Superstar*, the Andrew Lloyd Webber/ Tim Rice landmark musical, was scheduled to open at the Polk Theater of the Tennessee Performing Arts Center on May 12, 1988. The rock musical, depicting the last six days in the life of Christ, was the final show in the TPAC season. Staged initially in 1969, the hit had spun Webber's career into the big time. He hit again with *Joseph and the Amazing Technicolor Dreamcoat, Evita, Cats, Starlight Express,* and if those monsters weren't enough, *The Phantom of the Opera.* Now many felt it was time to explore Webber's roots again, and this Nashville show would do just that.

When it surfaced in 1971, *Jesus Christ Superstar* had sparked a nationwide controversy. Webber, and his lyricist, Tim Rice, presented Jesus as often confused, as well as a very undivine person. It was originally seen as a "hippie" version of the Gospel of Matthew and preachers and pundits sang out against it. A lot of this anger was created because Rice and Webber concluded their modern opera with no mention or hint of the greatest religious figure in the Christian world having risen from the dead and having been taken to Heaven to be with his father. Yet it not only endured, it became a hit. The Nashville version was going to clean up the hippie angles and play this latest version a bit more conservatively. In, Tennessee, Jesus was not going to bumble or fumble much; after all, this was the Bible belt, where the Ryman Auditorium had begun life as a church.

New York actors Eric Riley and Louis Padilla were brought south to play the leads, Judas and Jesus. Both had extensive experience on Broadway and in road shows around the country. Riley was even in the original production of *Jesus Christ Superstar.* Yet many of the other parts were going to go to local actors. So there would be a real Music City feel to the final production. To ensure this, casting calls were sent out areawide.

Pam first heard about the auditions for local talent through the Nashville musical grapevine. She even considered calling and trying to audition for producer Mark Pirkle herself. After all, her country music career was dead in the water, and here was a chance to be a part of something different. She had actually admired the musical for years, besides having long told people how much she admired Pirkle and his work. One of her personal goals had been to be able to meet the producer/director. She had said for the past year that anyone who could make theater profitable in Nashville had a great deal going for him. Yet in spite of all of her enthusiasm about the musical and the man behind it, trying out for a part was not really in her plans. She would leave that to the professionals. She had jingles to sing!

Renee Grant Williams could sense not only Pam's hidden desire to make a play for a part in the production, but she also felt fully confident that Pam had the talent to land one of the most important roles. She even called the musical's casting representative and told them to keep an eye out for her student. She then sent Pam on her way to meet the people in charge.

Even for old pros, auditioning for a producer of this magnitude always creates false hopes and expectations. In the face of these feelings, Pam was not going to allow herself to dream too much. She told herself she wasn't going to worry. No matter how badly she wanted to be in *Superstar,* she was simply going to walk in, give it her best shot, then let the chips fall where they may. Then if she didn't get a part, which was to be expected, at least the experience would be a good thing. At first pass, Tillis thought she had failed and pretty much put being in the musical out of her mind. Then she got a callback.

Pam was in L.A. when Pirkle called. They chatted about everything but the part for almost an hour. Then in a very casual manner, the producer finally got around to informing Pam that she would be playing Mary Magdalene. Pam couldn't believe it. She was so excited that she called everyone she knew to tell them the big news. She later joked that the money she spent on long distance calls was probably more than she was paid for the part.

As she came back into rehearsals, Pam was unprepared for her own feelings of inadequacy. It was simply overwhelming to work with people who could sing, act, and dance. These actors knew every facet of the business. They understood what it took to make the whole thing work. They were much different than other musicians with whom she had worked in the past. They were complete.

She told writer Thomas Goldsmith, "In the music business, you only see one dimension of people." Yet here she was working with people who could do it all. This was a long way from coming out, playing three chords on a guitar, saying "Howdy," and cutting loose with a few songs. Yet even the fear of having to learn so much so fast didn't faze Pam for long. She quickly got into it, pushing herself to feel the part, to expand to meet the challenge. She soon found herself thinking about it every moment. It almost consumed her. And this was exactly what Pam needed, something to engulf her to the point of getting her to dive in and give it her complete attention.

From the first day, Pirkle could soon see that his instincts in choosing Tillis has been right. Perhaps it was because she was so new to the field, but she seemed so vulnerable. This was the way he viewed Mary Magdalene, and so the two very different people from very different times quickly become one on stage. The same way Mary had been transformed by the power of Jesus and his effect on her life, Pam had been transformed by the way that she saw this woman. It was a transformation that would have very powerful results.

In a May 12 story in the *Nashville Tennessean*, Thomas Goldsmith chose to feature Pam in his preview of the musical. A very honest Pam informed Goldsmith, "There's not the first bit of dialogue, but there's musical dialogue. And I have always been real aware that in a song every line can be sung a million different ways.

"I've always approached it [music] like an actress, I think." Her new thinking and appreciation could really be noted when she added, "It's just colors, playing with different colors."

During the musical's ten-day run, Pam got to really experiment with the emotions and story-telling potential of the music. She had long held that the most important element of country music was the lyrics. Yet in reality what drove much of the music that was selling in today's market was the beat. People were once again dancing to country music and this was changing the importance of the words. This was something that a woman who revered the work of tunesmiths hated to see. She wanted everyone to know and understand each song's special message. As Mary Magdalene in the story of Jesus, there was a message that needed to be told and she gave it her whole heart. When she was on stage, she was Mary, and the producer felt that the crowd sensed this at every show.

Yet Pam's desire to do the best work of her life was wrapped around more than just her love of this part. Pam had also developed a huge respect and admiration for those in the cast and crew. She knew that she was a mere amateur in their eyes and that this production meant a great deal to each of them. If she messed up, it would make them look bad. In Pam's case this simply meant going back to writing at Tree. In the case of many of those in the cast and crew, it might mean losing a chance to get another job in the business. This feeling of having to reach a high standard for the sake of the others added to the pressure Pam felt as she worked. She would give it everything she had.

Most country music people didn't expect a great deal from Pam. A Tillis in a Broadway production has a certain "country bumpkin" feel to it. Yet in the May 13, 1988 *Nashville Banner* Beth Monin gave the musical superstar high marks. She wrote, "The Tennessee Repertory Theatre took a musical that the skeptics said couldn't be resurrected and brought it kicking and singing back to life." Then Ms. Monin noted what the "country bumpkin" had brought to the stage.

"Playing the role of Mary Magdalene, Pam Tillis nearly stopped the show. The daughter of country great Mel Tillis and a recording artist in her own right, she brought to Mary a natural soulfulness."

Those kind words would have been enough to have thrilled Pam, but Ms. Monin didn't stop there. She added, "Now tinged with a country ache, later with a shattering soul music wail, Tillis's magnificent voice made new even the too-often heard 'I Don't Know How to Love Him.'

"And the electricity doesn't fade away 'til long after the curtain has come down."

A day later the *Nashville Tennessean*'s Clara Heironymous gave the musical a top flight review too. Writing about Mel's daughter she remarked, "As Mary Magdalene, Pam Tillis makes an auspicious stage debut. Her singing has an underlying melancholy, neither blues nor country, but beautifully tender and bringing the right edge of 'I Don't Know How to Love Him.' This role does not call for much acting, but clearly she [Pam] understands the mood."

Yet when the musical ended, so did Tillis's temporary repast in solid and gainful employment. The party was over and Pam's life was once again centered on the latest song idea, cutting demos, trying to track down record labels who might need a new female artist, and identifying just who she really was and how she fit into the world of entertainment. Some days she was flying to Chicago doing auditions for commercials and thinking about looking at the money in acting. Other days she was wondering if she had a chance on the New York stage. In reality, she was doing anything that offered her a chance to work in show business. She was focusing on everything that offered a creative outlet, and discarding no opportunities, no matter how remote. If she found a door, she knocked.

Meanwhile, Mel's life had really taken off in Missouri. His show and his theater were a hit, and he was ready to offer Pam a job in Branson. Like so many others, Mel had almost given up that country music in Nashville was ever going to recognize his daughter's talents. Still, even though times were tough and Pam recognized that Branson was exploding, she didn't want to go there. She may not have had a record deal, but she still had her pride. She wanted to make it on her own, not by riding Dad's coattails. Of course making it anywhere was going to be hard right now. Not only did she not have a record deal, she did not even have a manager.

Chapter Eight

As Pam Tillis faced having to rebuild her career from the ground up, Sally Schloss of the Country Music Association's *Tune-In* wrote, "She has all the right ingredients for success: arresting good looks, a powerful full-bodied voice, fresh, well-crafted songs, and kinship with a country music legend. So why, with her extraordinary talent and presumed connections in the business, has Pam Tillis never gotten the big break?"

Schloss concluded her look at Tillis by adding, "If she ain't ready now, nobody is!"

Schloss's overview notwithstanding, Pam was anything but alone. There were a long list of talented acts who had worked their tails off, put out good records, and spent years on the road, only to watch others with less talent win over the fans and the disc jockeys, as well as make the millions of dollars in royalty payments and concert sales. Certainly Louise Mandrell could be considered as unfortunate as Ms. Tillis. While not a writer like Pam, Ms. Mandrell had one of the most electric shows in the business. She was good-looking, personable, dynamic on stage, and a performer who constantly challenged herself and continued to grow, but she couldn't get a real break. Like Pam, a big part of Louise's problem might have been her last name. The fact was, coming out of the shadows was nearly impossible, and

Mandrell and Tillis were both swimming upstream as they tried.

So what was it going to take for Pam Tillis to achieve a bit of the status which many of Music City's most perceptive voices felt she deserved? How was she going to get that big break? Those who wrote the glowing words demanding that Pam be noticed had proposed no magic formula to set in motion a plan to meet their demands. The fact was that they didn't how to do it either and many were just as frustrated by their impotence in this matter as Pam.

The business of Nashville is country music. Country music had always been and was still being driven by recordings. Without a recording contract, an artist could only have limited success. If you were a veteran with a string of hits you could make a pretty good living taking your show back on the road and playing nostalgia-filled bookings. You could even stay in the public eye by doing the Opry. You could also go to Branson or one of the other small tourist meccas which had embraced country music as their theme. Or, like so many were still doing in Music City, you could appear on TNN from time to time, work local clubs, and hope that somehow, someone noticed you.

Pam had been around long enough to recognize the routes that were open to her. She also realized that getting a record deal and getting back into the business in a big-time way was going to be a problem. Worst of all, it was too late to get her father's help. All the folks that ran the business when he was at the top were gone. And time was running out too. In Nashville, women who hit forty were considered too old to promote. At this point some of the biggest acts in the business with great track records, like Barbara Mandrell or Loretta Lynn, couldn't get a record deal because they were considered senior citizens by the day's radio market. Music City was becoming more and more youth oriented and Pam was already in her thirties. So while it appeared that it was going to take some time to find a label interested in giving her another chance, Pam also had to wonder just how much time she had left before labels ceased to be interested in her at all, or if a label would even give her enough time to build a career.

One suggestion that many of her friends made was to get back on the road full-time and get to know the country music fans up close and personal. This meant working small fairs, smoky clubs and little civic centers, or opening for acts that had had a hit record or two in the last few years—acts which were somewhere between obscurity and Decatur. Pam remembered her father doing just this type of road work for so many years. When she thought about how long he had been away from home, how much she hadn't been with him, she knew she could not rebuild her career this way. She simply wasn't going to do this to Ben. In her mind, her son had to be more important than her career. It had always been that way and always must remain that way. This was a rare, almost foreign, kind of thinking in Nashville where music usually came before everything.

So while Pam could have been and probably should have been charging out to do 300 dates a year, riding a large silver bus across miles of nothing, and building a foundation for a huge fan core in towns that didn't even have a motel, she stayed mainly in Nashville and chose to work at her own pace. She even had the courage to publicly admit that while she admired Reba McEntire, she wouldn't want to work like she did. That kind of life of touring and constantly pushing the limits didn't appeal to her. She had seen the road and didn't like that kind of life.

"I don't want to see the world from a hillbilly bus," she told those who explained that this was the only way to resurrect her career. As she began to analyze the price that everyone wanted her to pay, she even began to question her own choice of careers. She told *Tune In*'s Schloss, "I did music all my life. I said when I was little that I wanted to be a singer before I even knew what a pain in the butt it would be. I guess I never really thought about being anything else. I question that as an adult.''

While she was rethinking her own choice of vocation, it didn't mean that she didn't admire and respect those who had gone before her and done the very things that she didn't really want to do now. While Pam didn't want to hit the road constantly like Reba was doing, when she looked around the industry, her role models were largely women who had done the same thing.

One whom Tillis respected deeply was Loretta Lynn, a female who wrote her own music and gave women a real voice. Pam liked the way that Lynn had been outspoken when it wasn't supposed to work that way. The legend's message made an impact as to what songs were supposed to do. They were supposed to preach and yell if that's what it took to be heard. They were supposed to say something and improve lives for people. Loretta had done that time and time again. She had made the world better for every other female act in the business and millions more at home.

Pam also pointed out to folks that Dolly followed Lynn and rolled the doors open even wider. Pam told those who would listen that Parton created the image she wanted and bucked any man who tried to control her. She became her own boss and established a business that became an industry. She lived her dreams in a big way. She went where she wanted and she sang what she wanted. There was a big brain behind the makeup, and any executive in Nashville who had underrated Dolly had paid for it. She had always come out on top, even when things got nasty.

Then there was Barbara Mandrell. Tillis loved Mandrell because she had such a strong focus on her career and she proved that a woman could make it in the dog-eat-dog world of network television. When girl singers were supposed to be cute and open for the big men stars, Mandrell did it all and proved herself to be the best performer in Nashville. She stood behind no man. When Barbara won the CMA's ''Entertainer of the Year'' twice, it was because she was the best entertainer in the business, not just that she was having a few good years.

The toughness of Lynn, Parton, and Mandrell might have been something which Tillis admired, but did she have it? Many questioned if Pam, who was known as being fair and sweet, had the kind of grit and resolve that it took to be a successful woman in a largely man's world. It seemed from the way that she phrased her answers in interviews that Pam might have even wondered about that herself. Did she really have what it took to make it? Was she even focused enough to make it?

While Pam wasn't doing much to impress or interest the labels, she still could help pull in strong television ratings. This became apparent when TNN, *Nashville Now,* and Ralph Emery opted to honor Mel with a night of his own. Ralph had found that viewers loved these theme and family nights, so the network pushed this one special evening for Mel in promotional spots throughout the week before the show aired. The elder Tillis came in from Missouri to Tennessee, while his kids popped in from their own homes. All the individual schedules were arranged so that the five children were there with Mel. At one point during the program the Tillis family members even performed together. Not only did the live audience eat it up, but the event caused remote control zappers to stop all across the nation. In spite of the fact that none of these Tillises were appearing on the Billboard charts and there hadn't been a big hit in years, TNN's special demographic group loved them. This show would become one of the highest rated in network history.

Mel was justifiably proud and still speaks of that evening. This ratings blitz was good public relations and promotion for his new Branson show, gave him a chance to look very fatherly, and was a way to show those in the music industry that he still had some drawing power left. Nashville's major labels had written off Mel long before. He was considered as out of date and as out of style as *Hee Haw.* Yet here he was, drawing better numbers for TNN than any of the young studs who hit *Nashville Now* on a regular basis. Just like the title of one of his old hits, Tillis was now extracting his own sweet "Mental Revenge." But in truth, it couldn't have happened without his kids.

The reunion was nice for the whole family. It was a good way to relive some old memories and make some new laughs. Yet it didn't offer much of a boost for Pam's career. The only thing it really accomplished was to show a few folks that she was still out there and she still had some talent. Nationally she wasn't dead, but she just might have been on life support. As Marty Stuart once said about his career, "I knew I needed work and help when I not only didn't have a label, but the buzzards were circling over my head." Pam just might have been feeling the same kind of emotions about that time.

Ms. Tillis was still a good draw in local Nashville area clubs. Those who came out to see her once usually did so because of their curiosity about Mel's daughter. Yet those who came back a second and third time did so because she was becoming a really good showman. In the past, Ms. Tillis might have just said a few words between songs and rushed through her show, but now she visited, displayed her great sense of humor, and let the audience get to see a lot of the genuine and honest charm that had never been lost on Music City's best journalists. Finally, this was the real Pam Tillis. The one who had earned such raves. While no one could believe that this confident stage veteran would still be backstage pacing and nervous before each show, what everyone did know was that Pam gave it her all every time she went out. And she did this even if the crowd was small.

At that time, one of Pam's live favorites was a women's song she had written, "Going to Work." Pam would often explain the song's meaning before she sang it. As she spoke of the number's deeply personal lyrics, many wondered if she wasn't talking about something from her own life. She described "Going to Work" as a story about a relationship that had gotten strained and harsh. The poor woman's only escape was when she went to a job she did well. She further explained that anyone who lives on the road, such as country music stars, shared in the song's message.

Pam's relationship with the country music industry had often been strained and harsh. She had been forgotten and at times abused. Her good work had either been overlooked or set aside. Yet in the face of all the rejection, she kept going back to work. She did so because she felt she did her work well. Those who caught her at this time usually agreed. She was now doing her work, even if it was only being noticed by a few people, better than she ever had before.

In the interview with *Tune In*, Tillis told Schloss, "As a writer, your main job is baring the heart. I've done a lot of cowriting—I'm trying to come to grips with the idea of writing alone—and the idea that, hey, they may not like it. A writer has to have a lot of ego in order to survive."

Writer/performers like Steve Earle could understand Pam's schizophrenia. Part of her was an artist, the other part a businesswoman. She was constantly at war with herself. It was almost like a fight to the soul. Should she be commercial or should she unleash the pain in her heart? Real songwriting was all about the latter, yet Nashville's new age songwriting had more to do with hooks than experiences. It was often more gimmick than soul.

With the personal nature of her songwriting in mind, it had become obvious that Pam needed a forum where she could take her experiences and share them on her own terms. She also needed a support group to help her accomplish this mission. She found both at an event that she created for one of Music City's most unique night spots.

The Bluebird Cafe often had special evening shows where the small club opened its stage as a showcase for songwriters. Now the writers who were invited to the Bluebird were not simply struggling scribes trying to find a place to publish their work. This was a not a stage which catered to starving artists. By and large, those who came to the Green Hills club were up-and-comers. The club prided itself on featuring the creators of tomorrow's hot sounds.

Unlike many of the area's night spots, the Bluebird Cafe was not large and it was not a tourist trap. The area around the cafe was filled with strip shopping centers. Just up the road were the private residential areas where many of those about to make it big in Nashville's business community lived. In many ways, Green Hills was a kind of stepping stone between the poverty of downtown, run-down urban living and the mansions of Bellmead. By the same token, the Bluebird Cafe was often a stepping stone between writing and getting taken seriously by the labels as a performer. And because of its often serious atmosphere, on most nights, the cafe was almost a listening room. If you were looking for a party, this was not the place to come. If you wanted to evaluate songs and singers and their potential, this was a great place to spend a few hours.

Pam helped put together a night called "The Women in the Round." Ms. Tillis hosted and invited three of her best friends in the writing business to join her. The first in this special quartet was Ashley Cleveland. Cleveland, who, like Pam, had also made some side trips into rock music, had known Tillis during the latter's brief stay at the University of Tennessee. Since that time Ashley had also tried to carve out a career in show business. Her most obvious contributions were as a songwriter. Some of her original compositions included "End of the Long Goodbye," "You Can't Walk the Wire," and "Take a Walk Through Bethlehem."

Tricia Walker was the next female scribe on the Bluebird's bill. Tricia had managed to compose a long list of published tunes. Included among these was "Halfway Around the World," "I'll Do the Best With What I Got," "Love Waits," "Ride This Train," and the southern anthem that had become a universal performance favorite, "That's What I Like About the South."

The final member of the foursome was Karen Staley. Karen had the longest and most impressive list of tunes to her credit. Many of Ms. Staley's songs had taken some long rides on the charts. Some of these, such as "Anchor Deep in the Ocean of Love," "He Thinks He's James Dean," "Hearts Breaking All Over Town," "Keeper of the Stars," "Let's Go to Vegas," "Lonely Days and Lonely Nights," "Mountains on the Moon," "She Took It Like a Man," and "Wicked Ways," she shared with an audience that listened when she performed with an almost rapt attention.

As the evening wore on, the four women joked, told stories, passed around a guitar, and sang their songs. The feeling was so intimate that it was like being in a living room. The performers were not nearly as aware of the audience as they were of each other. This one-time-only event was greeted with so much enthusiasm that it became a regular part of the Bluebird Cafe schedule for some time. And those who heard about the quality of the "Women in the Round," often rearranged their schedules just to catch it. Of course, with the limited seating and the house rules, interested parties had to get there early just to get a seat.

As 1989 gave way to 1990, Pam was having a good time and her "Women in the Round" series was beginning to get noticed by the right people again. Some folks who had given up on her as a performer were now taking a second look. The singer couldn't help but be happy when Highway 101 spent twenty weeks on the charts and peaked at number 14 with Pam's "Someone Else's Trouble Now." The song was a final hurrah for the group's lead singer Paulette Carlson. She was now out seeking to travel the highways on her own, so the timing for the hit couldn't have been better. Yet an optimistic Carlson was about to find out something Pam already knew—there was only a limited amount of room out there for female artists. Carlson would not produce near the sales or gain near the exposure as a solo act as she had with her group.

Yet even as Paulette stumbled, Pam seemed to be finding

her balance. She was getting some press again and she had landed a manager, Mike Robertson. When he had quizzed her about goals, he pleasantly discovered that she now had some rather specific ones.

Pam informed Mike that she had five career objectives which she wanted to have happen in the near future. Without accomplishing these five things, she felt that her potential as an artist would be wasted.

First of all, Pam wanted to be signed by a record label. In the past, she might have taken any label. This time she had a certain imprint in mind. She wanted a contract with Arista Records. This choice would have seemed strange for anyone who didn't know who was behind the label. At that time, Arista was a company in name only at that point. The label had no country music experience. They didn't even have a Nashville office. The buzz on them was only strong because they had hired Tim DuBois, a songwriter and Music City wonder boy, to establish the label in Music City. Tim was riding high, having just cowritten the song that had established Vince Gill. ''When I Call Your Name'' had become a huge hit and had a lot of folks calling Tim's name. He responded to one of those calls when he got the chance to get together with Arista. Pam's knowledge of, respect for, and trust in DuBois moved his new label to the top of her wish list.

The next thing Pam had to have was something that her father already had six of, a number one record. For an artist who had never even cracked the top forty, this was quite a goal. Considering she didn't as yet have a record deal, it seemed almost implausible. Yet she was resolute about it.

With no contract and no hits, Pam's next step to success really seemed like pie in the sky. She told Mike that she wanted to have a gold album. It seemed that if Mike was just going to help her make these first dreams come true it was going to practically take an act of God. Who could have blamed him if he had been a bit nervous when waiting for the final two goals. He might have even been wondering if Pam wanted to somehow become the Queen of England. As it turned out, all she really wanted to do was perform at the Grand Ole Opry as a solo act and be a celebrity guest on a TV fishing show. Mike figured that it might be best to start with one of those last two. They were the easiest ones.

Meanwhile, as Pam set to work defining and shaping her next few years, some of Paul Worley's tapes of Tillis's work were to be noted by the label she so badly wanted to call her own—Arista-Nashville. Tim DuBois needed artists who were special and could provide a jumpstart for the label. His problem was that most of the known and proven talent had already been signed by the major labels. Tim was either going to have to grow his own talent, which could take a while, or rediscover someone whose real talent had gone untapped. When he heard Pam's tape he sensed that he might have just found what Warner had somehow missed. Not wasting any time, he arranged a meeting. For Pam Tillis, goal number one was in sight!

Chapter Nine

The song "Melancholy Child" by Pam Tillis and Bob DiPiero had not made much of an impact on the charts when it was released by Warner, but the song's words did hit close to home in the Tillis household. Pam had an emptiness, she was considered a bit wild by her father and the Music City establishment, and she was trying to run from who she was. Yet for years this restless musical journey to find inner peace and worldly success hadn't taken her anywhere. Finally, as 1990 wound down, it looked as if Pam was going to have a chance to really outdistance her own melancholy child. As she signed her record deal, many believed that it was finally her time to shine!

After years of feeling ugly and unattractive, Tillis seemed to be more than a little amazed that the world now saw Pam as beautiful, exotic, and even sexy. It is no exaggeration that this was a thrill for a woman whose face had once been crushed in a car wreck and had been worked on seemingly countless times by some of the nation's best cosmetic surgeons. As she would tell her friends, it was better to bloom late than not at all. Yet Cinderella feelings of going to the ball were not the only thing which had Pam feeling as if she was blooming in a garden of promise. The career "thing" was now being looked at differently, too. Just like she was suddenly being considered physically alluring, there was an alluring quality about her professional opportunities at this time too!

The catch phrase of the day was "Ncw Country." Thc artists who were taking this form of music to the masses were young folks who might have been raised on rock, but were now being "hip" by playing Music City. Not only did these folks bring outside and, in some case, irreverent influences into the recording industry, but they also brought a gaggle of new fans who had never heard of folks like Mel Tillis or Buck Owens. Most of these new country music listeners didn't even know what *Hee Haw* had been or where Branson was. These kids had just recently discovered the country music genre, and a large part of that introduction had come not from their parents or the Opry, but via CMT and video.

Video was the most important revolution in country music since radio. And it was the new country acts who were really using it to its full advantage. Just like Ricky Nelson had once used the forum of *Ozzie and Harriet* to launch each of his new singles for Imperial Records by debuting them each week at the end of an episode, now these young country acts were turning their best sides toward the camera and exposing a new batch of youngsters to the craze of teen idols through mini-movies that ran countless times on CMT. Unlike the fifties when the music of choice had been cleaned-up rock and roll, this time the music was hard-driving country. And the hunks that were reigning in this new demographic group were opening the door for folks like Pam, too.

On records, in concerts, in clubs, and on video, a host of country artists were now mixing music that encompassed all of the threads of rock, country, bluegrass, and R&B. Yet, while country music might have just caught onto this mesh of sound, Pam had been doing it for years. Not only did she feel at home in this world, she also had to feel like she had been the decorator who designed it. She had been there first. And almost everywhere she turned she heard what she had been trying to do for years. Only now it was selling. And because of that, a writer's writer had now begun to emerge as a singer's singer.

Armed with her Arista contract and a chest full of hopes, Pam hit the road with her band, the Mystic Biscuits. As was true of so much of Tillis's life, even the band's name could be traced to something special and private in her own background. Mystic Biscuits was a tribute to her mother. It seemed that her mom would talk about her latest psychic experience while making breakfast each morning. This was one of those experiences from her youth that Pam not only felt was funny, but unique to her. Mom's breakfast had always been good and brought about some warm and wonderful moments. Pam was hoping her band would do the same! It wouldn't take long for her to discover that her latest recipe for success was truly her best.

As she moved from town to town and show to show, Pam was drawing more and more people. The crowds that turned out to watch her were often a bit hard to read. As the critics would note, Tillis's audiences seemed to be a mixed bag. There were kids who were into the new stuff like Garth and wanted to tear the place up and rock and roll all night long. Then there were also a lot of Mel Tillis's fans who were there to see his daughter and hoped to laugh a lot. In the middle of these two groups separated by an extremely large generational gap, Pam had people who bought tickets because they liked her musical edge and hated country music. She would often discover when she met the crowd and signed autographs after the show that there were also fans who had come who loved country music but wished her sound didn't have the rockin'/folk edge. In a sense, this was an audience which Pam should have had no chance of pleasing. Yet somehow almost all of them left feeling as if they had been given something special. A part of this was the confidence that was evident in Tillis's onstage enthusiasm and warmth. A bigger part of this fan love affair was that her music was better than it ever had been.

Few of those who now watched may have known this, but Pam was simply doing and building on what she had always done. Yet if you hadn't followed her fits and starts in the music business, you might have thought that she was combining the sounds of the country rock bands of the day, such as Diamond Rio and Restless Heart, while trying to maintain the girlish charm and appeal of a Lorrie or Reba. Some even saw her still as a rock star wannabe. But this was no longer in her long list of wishes. She didn't have to be the rock star to work the large venues and grab the young audiences. Everything she had looked for in rock music had now come home to country. Yet even as much as this change in the genre offered Tillis a chance to really spread her wings and fly, a part of Pam remained clearly glued to the ground. She had been around long enough to know just how many false starts there were in this business and the only thing she could really depend upon was her family. So even as her career jetted toward the stars at an ever-quickening speed, she still put her son first in her life.

Though it frustrated some who were pushing her career, Pam was sometimes late to press interviews simply because she felt it was her duty to make sure Ben was at school, at a game or other activity, or understanding his homework. Even when some public relations experts were telling her to do ten interviews a day to assure this "final last chance at stardom" wouldn't be a bust, Pam remained largely unmoved, turned down some interviews so that she could stay involved in almost every detail of parenting. Ben took precedent over everything, including her social life. She even set up her road schedule around his activities.

"I don't want to be a career women without love in my life," she would tell the media. Then she would add, "But I don't want to be a person without her own dreams." Many of her dreams involved Ben. Without him happy and secure, then accomplishing any or all of her goals didn't matter to Pam.

Another way that Tillis set herself apart from many artists who literally ate, talked, and slept country music was that she also found time for herself. One of her favorite activities was reading because it helped her put her own life into perspective. In early 1991 she was in the midst of digesting Carrie Fisher's book *Surrender the Pink,* and what Ms. Fisher was describing in the pages of her best-seller sounded a great deal like Pam's own story. After all, Carrie was the daughter of a talented woman and a superstar dad, and she had had to fight to be recognized in her parent's field.

Pam was so moved by *Surrender the Pink* that she even spoke about it during an interview with *Close Up*. For Pam, whose career was finally in motion and headed down a promising road, the book seem to place things into a vivid perspective. As she told *Close Up,* it was a "thing of having a powerful, absent father. The whole thing in the book is how it affects you." Tillis further revealed how in Fisher's book, the author described a bit of everything Pam has been through on her own. Both women had strong fathers whose personalities could dominate a room. Both turned to writing to express their emotions and feelings. Both had bad first marriages. And both gave of themselves and their fears in their work. As Pam spoke of Ms. Fisher's experiences, it was almost like she had discovered a soul mate. One she hadn't met but seemed to know very well.

Yet there was a major difference in where Pam was and where the book's author was. For Carrie, the journey was on the downside; she had made it to stardom and earned her respect. Pam was just getting a real chance for that opportunity. In order to accomplish that goal, she was going to have to put together a hit album for the fledgling Arista label.

A now completely honest Pam used her own meandering search for musical acceptance to look for just the right cuts for her album. For years this search had been an often lonely quest, but now, thanks to Tim DuBois and the others at Arista, it was a team effort. They were going to find the best songs for Tillis and then give her the best money they had to offer in production and promotion. If there were gems to be discovered, they would find them. No longer would Pam just be a record label's afterthought; she was now a primary focus. This tremendous support had to give Tillis a boost like she had never known. For the first time ever, everything was first class!

Pam searched through hundreds of demos for the songs she wanted to cut, and no one at Arista got in her way. When she quietly let it be known that she wanted to be involved in every facet of her career, they said fine. And when the music was finally picked out and they put Pam in the studio, Arista did what few big companies ever did, they sat back, let Tillis work, and took in the results.

For those like DuBois, who had been around the business for a while, it was obvious from the first full day in the studio that this project was going to be special. Pam had been obsessive about her music for most of her life, and now she seemed to have a forum that allowed her own drive to set her sound apart from all the other music that was being produced in Nashville. Her time seemed to have finally arrived.

Put Yourself in My Place was the name of Pam's first Arista CD. The label felt that it was as perfect as a debut album could possibly be. From the first, Pam knew that her place was a good place to be!

The *Put Yourself in My Place* liner notes began ''First, I'd like to thank ahead of time, everyone responsible for making this my first gold album . . . But seriously, that's how much I believe in my team. Talk about a new start.

''Paul Worley, who got the ball rollin' in a major way. All the folks at Sony Tree Publishing with a staff too big to name and everyone who has been sweet and helpful to me on a regular basis. I'm grateful on a daily basis because I was lucky to hang there.''

Leave it to Pam to remember Paul Worley. When no one had wanted her and Warner had written her off, Paul had stepped in to not only support her as a songwriter, but as a friend and artist. His extra time producing and pushing her demos had now paid off in a big way. At the time Worley and Tillis first got together, no one but Pam probably felt that this would be a gold medal effort, yet it would be. And without Pam and Sony Tree, this incredible debut album never would have gotten off the ground and Tillis would still be mainly known as Mel's daughter and a former ''Stutterette.''

Pam also took the time on the notes to mention other Nashville talents who had proven that they would stick with her through thick and thin. Then Tillis, whose sense of humor was now well known around Arista, asked the question, ''Ed Seay—where have you been all my life? To think I've gone all this time without knowing the Leslie Gore factor.'' Even in the midst of her most important musical message, the Tillis humor came out via an inside joke. That is how comfortable Arista had made this experience.

Of course, Pam couldn't have made the album without the wonder boy Tim DuBois. He had taken the real chance and if it paid off, he would benefit. But if it didn't, he might well have to go back to songwriting instead of running a record label. Pam said of him, ''And, last but first, Tim DuBois who's keeping his promises and ain't it funny how things come around?''

Yes, most would have to admit as they listened to the album that it was funny how things do come around. Certainly Pam's time for stardom looked like it might have just arrived. And surely all the musical facets that she had embraced over the years had now come to Nashville and become a part of the new Music City sound. And a lot of the naysayers had come around, too!

Finally, Pam thanked the most important man in her life.

She wrote, "And Ben for keeping my priorities straight."

As the album was shipped, Tim, Pam, and the remainder of the folks at Arista sent up a few prayers and crossed their fingers. It was tough for any new label to make it in Nashville. MTM had tried a few years before only to leave town with their tails tucked between their legs. A few others had suffered the same fate. Arista would need to quickly capture some of the magic that the company had known in rock to make this work in Music City. As the reviews came in, the label decided that Pam had answered their prayers and brought them some much-needed luck too!

New Country Magazine wrote, "Tillis's Arista debut promises great things from its very first line—'She broke your heart in two million pieces.' " The reviewers here gave it three and a half stars.

The next review that came in was just as positive and much more important. *USA Today* called the album, "an invigorating introduction to the crystalline vocals and rock-solid material of Tillis's new album, *Put Yourself in My Place.* It's a package loaded with personality and wit and the high gleam of experience."

Who would have believed that even the tough voice of *Entertainment Weekly* would chime in that "Pam Tillis has now placed herself among country's most accomplished modern women."

As pleased as Pam was with the reviews, she was even more pleased with the way it sounded when she listened to it. It really felt like her. It was really true to her musical goals.

"There is one thing I can say about this record," she told the press through an Arista public relations release. "It's pretty honest, because I'm one of those people who believes that there's two sides to everything. So, this album is about the weak and strong sides of love. It's about the hurting and the hope. In fact, at one point, I wanted to jokingly call it 'The Flip Sides of Love.'

"I started out saying I'm not going to make an album

of love songs. But I wanted to sing songs that really said something, that really felt good and these are the ones.''

The title cut had been cowritten with Carl Jackson, a man known as a superpicker who began his career in bluegrass at the age of 14. When still a teen, he worked with Glen Campbell where he played banjo, fiddle, guitar, mandolin, and dobro. He recorded for a while, with limited success, and then worked with such acts as Vince Gill and Emmylou Harris. His songs had been cut by Glen Campbell, Wild Rose, Ricky Skaggs, The Whites, The McCarters, the Nitty Gritty Dirt Band, Mel Tillis, and Johnny Paycheck. He had also worked sessions with the likes of Alabama, Steve Wariner, Steve Earle, Roger Miller, Ricky Skaggs, Paycheck, Harris, and Campbell. Initially, Pam and the writer had simply gotten together to share ideas. Those ideas came together as they penned a tune called ''Don't Tell Me What to Do,'' a musical story about someone who loved a hurting man and was willing to invite him into her life.

As the title cut climbed the charts, Pam climbed back into a relationship. Now realizing that she and Bob DiPiero could work together and date, she let herself explore the possibility of giving love another try. The first time it hadn't worked out too well, but maybe now she was mature enough and settled enough to give it a fair shot. Besides, it was easy to find Bob, even on the road, because he was now working as the guitar picker in her band.

''Don't Tell Me What to Do'' entered the charts in late 1990. By February of 1991, it was in the top ten and getting close to number one on some charts. On Valentine's Day, convinced that her career was finally headed down a secure path, Pam headed down a new road, too. She married DiPiero. In the space of one week she would get a new name and have a record that hit number one on several national charts. In *Billboard,* ''Don't Tell Me What to Do'' would rise only to number five, but it would stay on the charts for twenty weeks.

For years, Pam had been begging the music industry, her

father, and a host of others to leave her alone and let her make her own choices. "Don't Tell Me What to Do" could have been her motto. Now, though, it simply represented the biggest thing that had ever happened to her. Arista single number 2129 had made her one of country's newest stars.

In the midst of putting her new marriage on the road to success and building her new fast-moving career, Pam was in the midst of lots of press interviews. On top of that, she was nominated for the CMA "Horizon Award" and was scheduled to make an appearance too.

"I figured the Horizon thing was a trial by fire," she had laughed about her biggest—up until that time—national television gig. "If you can do the show without falling apart, they let you stay in the business for another few years." After a giggle, she added, "It was a big test. I kept telling myself, 'Now Pam, you belong here. You've worked for this, you deserve to be here, or you wouldn't be here.' I had to keep reminding myself that I fit in, that I'm good enough."

Tillis really did deserve to be there. After all, she had not only scored with "Don't Tell Me What to Do," but had followed that first Arista hit single with another, "One of Those Things." "Things," which had originally been a part of her Warner sessions, also landed in the top ten in 1991, peaking in the summer at number six.

The night of her first Country Music Association awards show, she chose to sing a number that had been released in late August. Of all of the Arista releases, "Put Yourself in My Place" would be one of her biggest charting disappointments, hitting only number 11. Yet because it was the song she sang on the same stage where her father had been honored so many years before, the number would have deep significance for Pam. And as she hit her mark that evening, she was a pro in full possession of herself and her skills. It was not obvious to anyone that she had spent the day meditating and praying she wouldn't hyperventilate. Yet she was scared. After years in small honky-tonks and clubs, Pam was now singing in front of folks like George, Loretta, and a dozen of country music's biggest legends. On top of that, thirty million people were tuning in that night. Most of them were potential fans and many were seeing her for the first time. In a very real sense, all the insecurities of her youth and her long unsuccessful ride in music came back to visit her in the moments before she walked on stage that night. And she had to face them, as well as leave them behind.

"I had to drop a lot of emotional baggage," she told *Close Up* about her journey to finally earn some success. "[I had to leave behind] a divorce, coming out of a family that wasn't normal, being lonely, being a single parent, all of those things. And I mothered my mother for a long time, too. That took up a lot of time." But Pam's time was here now, and on that show and in that moment she performed as well as she had ever done. She wowed the crowd and turned the place upside-down. Travis Tritt would win the award, but Pam won over the crowd! Arista, Bob, and even Mel couldn't have been more pleased or proud.

As Pam grew, so did those around her. The mother whom she had mothered had now become someone who was a pal. As Pam acknowledged to *Close Up,* "Mom's this whole other person—this really incredible, artistic, inquisitive, curious, intellectually open person that I never even knew existed. And I could've benefited from her being that person at an early age." Yet, as she hit the road more and had to share parenting with her mom, she realized that she was benefiting now too.

And Pam also admitted something else to the official magazine of the CMA. "Dad did a whole bunch of stuff right. And so he's a model of what to do business-wise." As she was becoming successful and known on her own as an artist, she began to use what she had seen her dad use to build that all important fan base. Just like Mel had learned from Minnie Pearl the formula of how to treat the fans, Pam had learned from Mel. And it was still working wonders on the road!

In all honesty, Pam's success and the success of her album were a tremendous boost to the new label. A new as they were, Arista needed someone to really come out of the gate with a hit. With her initial release, Pam had given them just what they needed. Now they could spin off to their other acts the momentum that Tillis had helped create. Pam had made them look like geniuses, and they were cashing in big time.

Pam, who had once talked about not wanting to see the world from a hillbilly bus, was now doing just that as she drove from date to date. And because she was spending so much time out doing bookings, she was having to depend upon her extended family, including her mother and father, as well as siblings, to help with her son. Ben was now twelve and even though he was well adjusted and independent, Pam realized that he still needed Mom around. It practically killed her to have to visit on the phone and find out about things secondhand. The fact was, no matter how well things were going on the road, she missed Ben all the time. And because she hated being away from him as much as she did, she got involved in the guilt shopping bit. This was not unlike what Mel had done with her. Yet even though Pam was spending a lot of time away from home, she didn't have to feel too bad. Bob's influence as a stepfather more than made up for Pam's time away. It was the balance that their home life had been missing for so long and had so badly needed. And even in the midst of having to give so much to her career, she had given this most important gift to her son.

As her records continued to hit the charts, and as Arista made plans to get her back in the studio, Pam tried to maintain a normal life in a normal neighborhood when she wasn't on the road. Yet as the fans began to seek her out, this became more and more difficult. Now it was hard to get through a meal without signing an autograph. Shopping at the mall was a challenge too! Pam was now finding out that being a star was even an bigger challenge than just trying to get people to notice her had been in the not-so-distant past.

And noticing they were! Country music was now so hot that NBC had decided to spotlight the genre on a weekly show called *Hot Country Nights.* And it wasn't aimed at the same market that had tuned in for *Barbara Mandrell and the Mandrell Sisters.* This series targeted the growing youth market that was making country their music. Hence, folks like Jeff Foxworthy were brought in because his brand of country humor was hot. Alabama, Clint Black, Lorrie Morgan and a host of other new country acts were there each week making music with even newer up-and-coming stars such as Mark Chestnut and Doug Stone. Oldtimers like Kenny Rogers were coming back some too, but mainly this show was about what was happening now. So that network tossed out the welcome mat for Pam Tillis, thus labeling her as the best of the new fresh country music voices. Her performance proved that she was too!

When 1991 began, Pam had a record deal, five goals, and a bit of hope. By the end of the year, Pam was a star who had already met a majority of her career goals. Tillis had hit gold with "Put Yourself in My Place," and had topped out on some charts with "Don't Tell Me What to Do." She had also performed as a solo act on the Grand Ole Opry in the spring. The fishing show was the only thing she hadn't managed to hook. But that might just have to wait, because at this time, she had even bigger fish to fry!

Chapter Ten

Having started her Music City career at the same time as country music's two most important video outlets were launched, Pam Tillis knew the real value of CMT and TNN. From having spent so much time in front of audiences and then listening to the fans after the show, she also knew that the two cable networks were the best public relations tool she had. So Pam took full advantage of using Ralph Emery, Crook and Chase, and any other video forum in pushing her music. This push helped the attendance at her live shows more than she could even measure. In the old days it had been word of mouth and radio, now it was cable and video. And as anyone who had seen her work in music videos knew, Pam was a master of the creative use of video presentation too. She had always sold a song through its story. Perhaps because she was so steeped in rock music, the video medium was therefore made to order for the young talent.

If you had a creative, fun, or touching video, then you had an opportunity to reach people and turn them on to more than just your music. A good video could also turn them on to you. Pam had seen Reba McEntire not only transform her image through the use of video, but build a huge career. This was the wave of the future, but it was happening now!

In the past, an artist had no choice but to use live shows to let people see a bit of the real personality. That is how Loretta Lynn and Barbara Mandrell built their huge followings. In live shows, performers would get to people in a very personal manner and make them like them. It had worked so well too. Few shows drew more than a few thousand people and the concerts were somewhat intimate. After the show there was usually plenty of time for autographs, pictures, and talk, too. Now, with country music fans getting younger and loyalty largely a thing of the past, with shows drawing tens of thousands and autographs sessions largely becoming a thing of the past, video provided the instant gratification which most fans needed. If they liked what they saw of you in a music video, then they generally liked you, too. Hence, country music videos, which began a few years before as just bits and pieces of concert footage, had now evolved into mini-movies or mini-sitcoms, depending upon the message the artist was trying to send. In most cases, Pam went for the humor. And with the financial backing of Arista and their creative staff, she usually found the funny bone.

Video may have been one of the reasons that another evolution was beginning to take place in Nashville too. In the midst of an election year, a presidential candidate's wife told *60 Minutes,* "I'm not sitting here like some little woman, standing by my man like Tammy Wynette," and the buzz which Hillary Clinton heard after these ill-timed words may have cost her husband a few votes. Yet Bill Clinton, a Southerner who grew up listening to rock and had migrated over to country music, had been elected and this seemed to indicate to the world that the baby boomers were about to take over everything, so that meant change.

Ms. Clinton might have used the Tammy Wynette classic "Stand By Your Man," to make a point about her own personality, but she could have used it to point a finger at Nashville too. Ever since the beginning of the country music business, producers hadn't been able to stand a woman standing up for themselves. This was simply not the way it was done. Women's lib didn't work here, and if a woman tried to toss around too much weight, the genre put her on a diet or put her out to pasture. The fact was that the power base had long been white-collar redneck males. Up until this time, a woman's job in Music City was to tease her hair and her men. Women were supposed to be sexy and sing, then graciously say thank you for what little they got in return for all their hard work. The reality was that a few women could be marketed and make money, but they were to be given no real power.

Yet, strangely enough, women made up 80 percent of the country music audience. With that in mind, the male producers had always assumed that these women buyers wanted the same kind of musical message from their lady singers as they had received from Victorian romance novels. Right or wrong, such had been the thinking for generations in Nashville. Loretta Lynn was one of the few who had broken from this conservative view, and she had hardly started a revolution. She was a lone voice in a sea of women sticking by their man no matter what he did.

Besides the fact that women like Pam had to cope with the outdated notions of out-of-touch men when recording material, there was the even larger problem of radio airplay. Though most fans may have been women, most disc jockeys had been men. Throughout the 1980s, women only got about a quarter of the time on radio stations. By 1990, that time had dropped in half to only one-eighth. With more country music than ever being produced, there was less room for the glut of product. You simply couldn't expand one hour of music into anything more than one hour of music. Yet the hordes of men selling product didn't have to sacrifice. They got even more time while the women were having more and more precious minutes pulled from them.

A major cause for this was that country music had not yet fragmented on radio. In rock there were several different formats that allowed a lot of acts to find their niche. In country, a station in a small town in Ohio was probably playing the same cuts as one in Los Angeles. In a place like Dallas, with as many as six or seven major country music radio outlets, all of them sounded pretty much alike. This limited access, along with the growth of the country music band sound, was squeezing a lot of folks out of the marketplace. Many of the old acts had already been booted out. Gone were Tammy, Loretta, Barbara, and so many other former superstar acts. They hadn't used up their talent or good stuff, the industry simply didn't have room for them. And there was not a great deal of room for the new ones either. Now, with a fresh audience that usually listened for a certain style, not a certain star, it was the song which earned a spot on the playlist, not the artist. Gone were the days when a core of fans would guarantee an act like Conway Twitty or Sonny James twenty straight chart-topping singles. Each new cut had to be better than the last or it didn't fly.

The pressure to always have a winning song was much greater than ever before. Because of that, and the tremendous expense in pushing and producing an artist in the big business of country music, there was very little room for mistakes. A generation before, a label might give an artist five to ten years and twenty singles to develop into a star. Now you were lucky to get three singles over one year. If none of them made it to the top ten, you were gone. Therefore, the few chances that were given must be taken, and the most must be made of each of them.

Of course, there were rewards if you scored. Country music was now a huge money-making industry, and this could mean big bucks for an artist. Garth was making more money in a year than the entire industry had taken in just a generation before. Songwriters could retire on the royalties from just one number one. Of course, the cut for female acts was still too small to satisfy the huge number of acts trying out for stardom. But in the face of the hard road to the top for most artists, it wasn't all bad news.

Even though the speed might have been too slow for most, times were changing in record sales and concert dollars. In the early sixties, Patsy Cline's Decca label pushed for the legendary singer to earn 30,000 to 40,000 sales per single. Even in the early eighties, Barbara Mandrell was hard pressed to sell more than 100,000 albums. Now Reba McEntire, the Judds, Trisha Yearwood, Tanya Tucker, Kathy Mattea, Lorrie Morgan, and K. T. Oslin had all earned gold and platinum albums. Country women might still labor somewhat in the background and have to fight to earn the spotlight they deserved, but they were selling better than ever before. This had to be a good sign for Pam and every other new female artist.

Jimmy Bowen, who had believed in Pam for more than a decade and was seeing another producer cash in on the promising act, noted in 1991 that "In the last seven or eight years, women are getting control of the production, what songs they're going to sing. It's becoming their music." Yet many wondered why it had taken so long and why was this finally happening now?

In reality, while Patsy, Dolly, Loretta, Tammy, and Barbara had set the table, it was Reba who had blazed the trail. The redhead had slowly built a career and had taken over when Mandrell had lost the top female artist spot. As McEntire grew as an artist and performer, the college grad also studied how other women in other fields gained control over their own destinies. Emulating Barbra Streisand and others in Hollywood, the Oklahoman slowly took control over everything from bookings to her own image. She even demanded control over her material. Before any of the men in Nashville really understood what was happening, Reba had established her goals and had evolved into a powerful force whose sales allowed her to take full control of every facet of her career. She created a company and pushed herself, her music, and a host of other acts. In a decade, she went from selling 40,000 copies of an album, to six figures, then to seven. She also demanded and won the right to be a closing act over even the biggest male stars. In less than ten years, she had proven that women could sell, draw, and make executive decisions. This would make Pam's demands for the same kind of career decisions much easier for Music City to take.

Another change transforming country music and signaling good things for Pam Tillis was the new audience coming over from rock, as much male as female. The males were looking at female performers and buying their music too. No longer was it just female fans purchasing the music of the hunks. Now there was room for "hunkettes."

In spite of all the doors that had opened, in 1991 only two new female acts, out of the two dozen who released records, broke into the top 20 playlists. One was Trisha Yearwood, the other, Pam Tillis. So in a sense, country music was opening its doors to women only if they were extremely successful. Anything less than that spelled a quick ride to oblivion. The reason for this was that record companies, looking at reduced air time, were now viewing the chances of a female artist paying off as much less than a male. The risk was therefore not worth the investment. Hence, fewer than thirty percent of recording artists were women, and that number was actually shrinking even through the sales for many female artists were going up. Reba had managed to open a door of opportunity for women, but there were a small number of people in the club that actually were allowed to use it. Pam felt lucky to be a part of that club, but she didn't necessarily appreciate the rules that went with admittance.

Pam told the *Journal of Country Music*'s Paul Kingbury, "They say you've got to appeal to women. Fortunately, I can do that. I haven't had to make a conscious decision. You know, it's not like, 'Oh, I'm gonna pretend to be a woman's woman.' Some women are better with relating to other women than others naturally. But I don't know. They tell me it's a fact. I just believe in songs that tell the truth. And if you're a woman, you sing about your real experience and people are gonna know if it's honest."

In a very real sense, Pam had hit the nail on the head. Why did women have to sing a certain kind of song in a certain way for a certain audience, when men didn't have to? Yet besides Reba, Pam was one of the few voices to speak up against this artistic limitation. She didn't want to do Sylvia kind of "hook" numbers, she wanted to hit the heart. She cared about making music more than she cared about making money. This flew in the face of marketing at the time. McEntire was big enough to pull this off, but was Tillis?

When she visited with Kingbury,.she didn't stop with just the type of music that Nashville expected a woman to record. She hit the female image thing, too! She didn't like the "big-hair bimbo, housewife-next-door look" that most female country singers felt that had to become on stage.

"I've heard people say, 'Don't be too good-looking; you'll intimidate people.' Which is crazy, because I'm just your average kind of girl. But I don't know. I think the demographic is changing. I have women come up to me and say, 'My husband thinks you're so sexy. Would you sign [this autograph], Love, Pam Tillis?' Like they like it! They want to identify with somebody that their husband likes. So you tell me [what's going on]. I have no idea."

Pam might have claimed that she did not have an idea about the new fans and their desires, but she probably knew that she had a much better grip on these matters than did most of the Music City establishment. She also had to feel pretty good that it wasn't the establishment who was in control of her career either. Arista was the new kid on the block and didn't mind doing things the new way. Maybe this was why Pam took every opportunity she received to inform the press that while she might have been confused about the new female image, she felt incredibly lucky to be searching out how to develop and use it.

Tillis's relationship with the press, which had always been good, was now better than ever. Many scribes were pushing her every chance they got. Some of the bold writers were even stating in print that Pam might even reach the success platform that her father had once called his own. A few even felt she would go beyond Mel and challenge the likes of Reba. Yet Pam seemed to have other ideas. As she went back into the studio to cut a second Arista album, her sights were not set on her father, Dolly, or even Reba. She seemed to be more bent on setting her eyes on the career of Willie Nelson. Nelson had created his own sense of place. His music had his distinct mark on it. He was a singer/songwriter who was recognized as such. He couldn't be categorized and he was completely at ease with his own image. He could sing anything he wanted. This was what Pam really wanted for herself.

Pam told Michael Bane of *Country Music* as she readied herself for a real shot at the big time, "I think I'm in a pretty good place right now. I've made my peace with a lot of old ghosts."

And for Tillis these weren't just idle words. She really had come to grips with the past. She was even relying on her mom for home-cooked meals, honest talk, and some child care, and talking to her father about the business and what to do in certain situations. Mel even saved Pam some money by letting her use his tour bus. Yes, times had changed a great deal in the past thirty-five years. What had separated father and daughter at birth was now bringing them together as adults.

When Pam had been born, Mel had been on the road with Minnie Pearl. In a sense, Minnie had been there for Pam in the beginning by providing the paychecks that kept food on the Tillises' table. Minnie was also one of the folks who had first helped open the door for women in country music. So the country music Hall of Famer had been there for Pam as a woman even before Pam was born. In a very real sense, even though she had not been blessed with a great deal of sex appeal or talent, over the decades Ms. Pearl had become a vital part of the entire industry. She was a friend, mother, talent scout, and cheerleader. So when Minnie suffered a career-ending stroke in 1991, the stars of country music got together to wish her a speedy recovery in a special two-hour special. And they did it in style. Scores of performers from Ricky Van Shelton to Connie Smith, from the new hats to the mainstays of the Opry, crowded the stage to pay tribute to a woman they all loved.

One who was there on that night was a new star who just happened to be an old friend: Pam Tillis. Pam performed a special song, "Hats Off to Minnie," with Jim Stafford, Ray Stevens, and her father, Mel. The father/daughter were now united on national television, and while the cause was noble, the material was silly. Dressed in Minnie Pearl-type hats, they sang the ode, smiled, and took the applause.

In a sense, it was good to see the two generations together. Yet it was a missed opportunity for father and daughter to really show off their wares. Mel had long been recognized as one of the genre's great talents, and Pam was now being showcased as the future. It was too bad that the two of them didn't get to come together on something more meaningful for both country music and Minnie than a song about the ailing star's hat. It was also too bad that Pam got lumped with comedians rather than with serious singers. Still, the exposure was good for her career. It reminded a lot of folks that Pam was happening!

Back in the studio, Pam finished her new album, picked a single and set about shooting the photos for the jacket and liner. These jobs completed, she then penned the liner notes to the work she called *Homeward Looking Angel,* thanking friends, family, and fans for their support.

"*Hope.* That's what I feel as I write these lines.

"*Hope.* Gold or platinum look great on the wall, but I just hope that this is music that means something, that touches someone, that makes *you* happy.

"That's enough for me."

Pam wouldn't have to wait long to find out just how much this album would mean to so many. "Maybe It Was Memphis" made its debut on the single charts just before Christmas 1991. It would take off like a rocket and hold on to this ride until late in the spring of '92.

USA Today wrote in their review of *Homeward Looking Angel,* "You would never know Pam Tillis was country star Mel Tillis's daughter, given her strong rock sensibility and contemporary lyrics. Already a successful songwriter, Tillis appears (with this album) to hit her stride as a recording artist and stage performer. She had a rare debut hit in '91 with 'Don't Tell Me What to Do,' and her current single, 'Maybe It Was Memphis,' is at number 26 with a bullet in *Billboard* this week. She's about to join that far-outnumbered clutch of female performers who manage to find success through top-notch skills."

USA Today cut right to the point when it sensed that Pam was using her background and talent to carve a place in the crowded country music field. She was, the newspaper felt, coming around at the right time and selling the right product. Ironically, it wasn't the first time that she had tried to sell the same material. She had cut "Maybe It Was Memphis" back in her days with Warner. She had felt that it was a hit even then and had released it on her first Arista album. The song hit the charts just when her new album was released.

"I'm just glad my antennas were up that day," Pam explained as she remembered the day that the Michael Anderson song crossed her desk. "I gotta tell you, that demo sounded like a Billy Idol record, but I heard a country song in there. I don't want to say risky, but what I assumed would be pushing the boundaries of country. And I've really worked with that song for years to get it to a certain point. Sometimes, when you really love a song, you've got to work with it."

Pam had cried when she first hard the initial playback

on "Maybe It Was Memphis." Yet these were tears of happiness, not sadness. This was a moment she had dreamed of for so long and it seemed now that all of her career plans were falling in place. It was a moment to remember when everything was perfect, the song, the message, the singer, the arrangement, and the emotion. It was really the story of Pam's career pushed into a three-minute envelope of music.

Pam's song, completed by a wonderful and touching video, was nominated for the Country Music Association's Single of the Year. It also should have been her first chart-topping single. Yet Garth Brooks kept "Memphis" from going number 1. This was something that the former Oklahoma State football player was doing to do to a lot of folks. So Pam was in good company.

"Maybe It Was Memphis" really set people up to take note of the strong material on Pam's *Homeward Looking Angel* album. "Shake That Sugar Tree"—also denied a chance at being number 1 by Garth Brooks—and "Cleopatra, Queen of Denial," were two of the most powerful cuts on the CD and some of the best things cut by a female artist that year.

While Pam was hitting the big-time on the charts, she was still working clubs more than she was the big arenas. One of the places that used her talents was Cowboy's in Dallas. Another was the Crazy Horse Steak House and Saloon in Santa Anna, California. Writer Gene Harbrecht of the *Orange County Register* caught Pam there and was moved to write, "It wouldn't be inaccurate to say Pam Tillis plays a room with the energy and style of a Garth Brooks. It would be equally correct to say she works a room with the comic timing of a Jay Leno."

Pam's concerts usually lasted just over an hour. As she had when she was a rocker, Tillis dressed to dazzle. Most of the songs she belted out were geared to push her own career. Still, Pam did take a few moments each night to give tribute to the past by wrapping her vocal chords around hits by George Jones, as well as Mel Tillis. Not yet weighed down with a huge number of single releases of her own, Pam used the show's early sets to show off a blend of rockabilly, country blues, and old-time country music. She also mixed the music with a few quick jokes and one-liners. The crowds now seemed to love her for more than her humor and her songs. They liked her personality and the fact that she worked hard for them. She often joked that for as much as she sweated on stage her Indian name was Running Mascara.

Night after night the small but growing crowds danced, whooped, laughed, and yelled for more. This showcase style combined with her records sales was beginning to take her places she had once only dreamed about. The Academy of Country Music nominated Pam for "Female Vocalist of the Year." As the days grew closer for the nationally televised spotlight, Tillis joked to audiences about wanting the crowd to wish her luck. She wasn't asking for luck in order to win the award—Pam assured all that Reba will take home the trophy. Pam just wanted some luck in order to find the right dress.

Pam found the dress and used the spotlight to its full advantage. Deep down, she might have even held out some hope that the vote would split and somehow she would win the award. She didn't. But in this case, she would have had to admit that being nominated was really just enough. With the sales of the new album heading toward gold, she was building a career which would surely give her plenty more chances at this and a hat full of other awards.

It didn't take long for the nominations and the hits to pull Pam out of the small clubs and put her into some very bright spotlights. When opening for George Strait in the big houses and earning the wonderful exposure that went with these opportunities, Pam noted that these crowds were more like rock crowds that she had once wanted to play for, rather than old country crowds who had come out to see her father. Maybe she had found the audience that she was looking for back in her new wave days.

The Strait opening allowed Pam to be something she couldn't be on the stage of small honky-tonks, and that was a full-blown concert performer. At the big convention centers, she took the audience who had paid big bucks to see George and won them over with humor, style, and especially her unique, strong voice. Her forty-five-minute show spotlighted her own music and even those who hadn't cared who was on the bill with George were wowed.

As the crowds stood up and gave standing ovation after standing ovation, Pam told her friends that she felt real country music acceptance for the first time. She was no longer trying to prove herself in Nashville. She even informed *Country Music Magazine,* "I told people I was just going to make the best album I could make, an album that I thought other people would like but that I liked, an album that meant something to me, and then just let it go."

She was at the right tree at the right time and had come loaded with the right formula for success too! Overnight she had ceased being Mel's daughter and was now a star in her own right. It had happened so fast that even Pam had problems putting it into perspective.

"I don't think you can say anyone deserves it [fame and success]," she told *Country Music.* "There's just so much to it. There's luck. And there's destiny. And perseverance—but that's a given. I mean, everybody's doing that here. There's a level of people who've gotten to Nashville. But outside of that, there's a question of whether it's meant to be or not."

Fame and fortune have their mysterious qualities, and Pam told writer J. G. Wirt of the *Bakersfield Californian,* "I think I did what I'm supposed to do. I think I'm right where I'm meant to be. For the first time in my life my timing was good, my instincts were good."

Yet something else had to be there too, and that was talent. Pam had struggled for years for people to notice that she was a talent in her own right. Now, when people did take note, she seemed a bit surprised and taken aback. It would take a while for Tillis to get used to this fact. Still, with Bob beside her and Ben always ready for a quick fishing trip, reality was there, too. Besides, what Pam had really always wanted was not fame or fortune, she had wanted the right to fulfill her own potential in her own way. Hers had always been a quest for artistic expression. Like her idol, Willie Nelson, she was on course to get just what she wanted while keeping all the things that were important to her, too! In truth, she wouldn't have had it any other way!

Chapter Eleven

At the beginning of the decade when Pam had signed with Arista, she had set her goal on earning a gold album. Now three years later she had two gold albums that had produced five top-ten singles. "Maybe It Was Memphis," "Shake the Sugar Tree," and "Let the Pony Run," had even made runs into the top five, and even "Cleopatra, Queen of Denial" was destined to peak at number 11, and would become one of her signature hits because of the impact of the dynamic and humorous video treatment on the song. In a sense, it would become country music's answer to the cult classic by the Bangles, "Walk Like an Egyptian." Old King Tut would have been proud.

"Cleopatra, Queen of Denial," was born via a bad joke Tillis heard about Cleopatra and Marc Antony. The song's lyrics were based on Pam's own experience with dating a complete jerk. Visualizing Prince Charming while dating an ego-fed loser, the writer put herself in a position that almost every woman has known at one time or another. She was a romantic loser trying against all odds to win. Yet like Cleopatra, this lovesick gal was snake-bitten. While the experience itself was not funny, the video and song sure were. And that is why this video, complete with Pam as Cleo, worked. Tillis really sold the story of wasted infatuation in such a strong and yet humorous way that fans couldn't get enough of it. Even though ''Cleopatra'' was nowhere near her biggest hit, it might just have been the song that got almost everyone noticing Pam Tillis. It might just have booted her into a bit of country music royalty.

In the past, it was largely the country music magazines that had taken time to review Pam's music. *USA Today* had chimed in with some kind words too, every once in a while, but like most country acts, Pam was treated rather distantly by the mainstream press. Yet after *Homeward Looking Angel* had been on the market and produced a few hits, *People* magazine stopped and took note. Tony Scherman wrote, ''Pam Tillis, 34, is a dual inheritor: of an illustrious name (her dad, singer-songwriter Mel Tillis, wrote one of Nashville's greatest songs ever, ''Ruby, Don't Take Your Love to Town'') and of Mel's classic honky-tonk style—doleful lyrics, pedal-steel guitar, and bare-wire emotion.''

Thanks in no small part to ''Cleo,'' even in New York the media and fans were recognizing the younger Tillis as a star in the making. Despite the great press and reviews, and even though she was opening for the likes of Vince Gill and Alan Jackson, Pam still had some doubts. She had been on a long journey to find herself and her niche. The trip had as many downs as ups. The pain of this long journey could be sensed when fans heard the cut, ''Homeward Looking Angel.'' It really was autobiographical. The song was the story of woman who had been out in the world, tried almost everything, then gone back home to find herself and get ready to try it all again. It was hopeful, positive, and wise, something that Pam herself now seemed. It talked optimistically about the bond of love between parent and child. Yet there was an edge to it that made you wonder if everything would really work out all right. Maybe there was some heartache left in the angel's life.

While she may have had her doubts, the critics seemed convinced that Pam was on the right track and would stay there for a long time. *Country Fever* called *Homeward*

Looking Angel a real winner. The reviewer wrote, "Her second album for Arista establishes Pam Tillis as one of the most original new singers and songwriters on the burgeoning country music scene."

New Country added their praise. "With its blues-borrowed sexual connotations, [it] couldn't have been sung convincingly by anyone else." The magazine, which centered on the hottest sounds in the country music youth revolution, gave the album four stars.

Even though she was well on the way to becoming a major player in it, Pam wondered a great deal about this new Nashville. She liked the sound, but she had reservations about the way the fans and the business dealt with the stars. As she looked around, she noted a great many folks who had been on top just yesterday were now forgotten and off the playlists. It seemed like just a few hours ago that Randy Travis and Clint Black had taken the business by storm, and now they seemed to be old hat. Just last year, K. T. Oslin had been the new voice of women in country music, and now no one heard her. After winning CMA's "Female Vocalist of the Year" two years running, Kathy Mattea had seemingly disappeared, too! How long before Pam suffered the same fate and, more importantly, how could she avoid it?

"Dad's fans stayed loyal," Pam told *People* when she spoke of this disturbing trend of toss-away stars. "Nowadays, to stay in the top five, I gotta work my butt off, because there's always someone else coming along." As Pam analyzed this new country, she wondered if there weren't too many new artists and if there was enough room for all of them. Like Marty Stuart, Pam mused that the Music City of today was in a state of constant flux. She had come to the realization that transition was honored and history was lost. And this frightened the daughter of a country music Hall of Famer a great deal more than playing in front of ten thousand people.

Reaching back to her rock roots, Pam told *Country Fever*, "John Lennon once compared stardom to wallpaper—it's disposable. Sometimes I think it's the way our media is right now. People's attention spans are shorter than they used to be. There's not so much regard for people who've paid their dues and lasted. It's this fascination with the new. A lot of really great artists who have a lot to offer get tossed aside, and it's the audience that gets shortchanged."

Pam continued to voice her concerns about this mentality to *New Country,* "I've been in this business long enough to know that one day you can be in sync with it, and the next day you may be out of sync with it and you can't figure it out. That kind of frightens me.

"Sometimes radio can just decide not to play you anymore. You don't get a lot of second chances in this business. I've seen artists who have had a couple of misses and then, that's it, they're gone."

Tillis, maybe for the first time in her life, was now beginning to fear for her father's great legacy of work, as well as her own. Like a proud daughter, she was standing up and talking about the way things were when Mel had earned his shot at the big time—the way she seemed to want them to be now.

She remembered how Mel had worked successfully for sixteen years to get to the top. She concluded, "Country music used to have the most loyal fans in the world. I'm not saying they're not loyal today, but the regular country consumer is confused and they're inundated. I think they're almost stunned. You reach a saturation point. I worry about that a little bit."

Country music had moved into an era when it was much like the Wal-Mart supercenters. Sure, there was a lot of great stuff there and most of it may have priced right, but it was overwhelming trying to figure out how to find it. Many fans were so confused and frustrated that they were simply turning away from country music. Others were just buying the first thing that came along. It was no accident that places like Branson were booming. Here patrons had a sense of security. They knew the acts without a scorecard. It was visiting the old country store. There was no country store left in Nashville, except for the Opry.

In the modern world, the only way to really beat this new-star-for-a-minute system was to pay very careful attention to every detail of your career. Reba had done that. She was always working to give the public something new. She was improving her shows, pushing to find better material, giving "them" something to talk about. Most other artists hadn't worked this hard to stay on top. They hadn't pushed to grow. When they hadn't, they had fallen more quickly than they had risen.

One of the ways that Tillis wowed the fans was during her shows. It was more than her energy and music. She dressed to kill. While she didn't spend a small fortune like some acts did having fancy outfits designed, Pam did work to put together things that would set her apart and give her a style of her own. Her father had always told her the fans expected you to look nice. He always had, and she thought it made good sense for her to follow the old man's example. For Pam, both on- and off-stage, this meant setting her own look. Helping her was a close friend and seamstress, Lynn Kirakoffe. Kirakoffe was responsible for much of what Pam wore in concert, but unlike so many other stars who would spend tens of thousands on original, one-of-a-kind custom-made outfits, Pam shopped for her look at the mall, then turned many of her finds over to Lynn.

Tillis would find "normal" dresses and blouses and then have Lynn add stuff to them. When the designer finished her star treatment, the results looked as if they had come out of a whimsical show in New York. Part country, part fad, but all original, these clothes set Pam apart and caused many women to wonder where she shopped to get such wonderful clothes. Country music magazine even did fashion sections all about Pam and her look.

"You want the audience to know that you cared enough

to dress up for them,'' she told her band more times than they cared to note. And she worked hard to do this.

Maria Smoot, the hairdresser to country music stars such as Tanya Tucker, Rosanne Cash, and Trisha Yearwood, helped Pam create a tress look that set her apart as well. Pam's hair framed her face and made a look that seemed to hearken back to the simple glamour of Hollywood's Golden Age. Fans loved it and for Pam, who had once cringed when she glanced in a mirror, to be considered a beautiful trend-setter was a wonderful development.

Yet as important as the look was, Pam knew that what was really going to make or break her career was her music. So even as she pushed the singles from her second album, her thoughts turned to what she knew she had to accomplish with the next one.

She informed *Country Fever* that ''the men are singing to the women, but the women are singing for the women.'' With that in mind, she sought out songs that spoke to this targeted group.

The voice that women singers were giving women in country music was touching maybe the last unliberated segment of society—the rural or blue-collar woman. Pam, Reba, and folks like Mary Chapin Carpenter were becoming their voice. They were singing songs that mattered to them. This was a much different message than the kind of songs most country female singers were pitching just a few years before. Sylvia was selling songs about ''Nobody,'' Barbara was ''Sleeping Single,'' but now Reba was asking ''Is There Life Out There?'' McEntire's video hit of ''Is There Life Out There?'' pointed to the real power of the message the ladies of this generation of country music could deliver. The video, a mini-movie about a woman going back to college, spurred more than 40,000 women to go back to school and get their degrees.

In a very real sense ''Is There Life Out There?'' showed that country music could do more than entertain, it could inspire. Pam believed that the voice of inspiration for females had to be females. Women understood where other women were coming from and what their needs were. And Pam took this responsibility to heart.

Tillis told one writer, "I think the business is paying a lot more attention to women, but there are still discrepancies." These discrepancies upset Pam, as well as motivated her.

Tillis felt that it was a shame that women worked just as hard in this business, but made less money than the guys. She wanted to make as much as the men.

She pointed out that women were allowed fewer mistakes. It seemed to her that a label would keep a man around a lot longer than a woman. She had seen this proven time and time again. Guys would have three of four bad releases in a row and still keep their deal. A woman who fell out of the top ten two times would be dead.

Pam was also upset by the age discrimination that was obvious on radio playlists. Men were in their prime when they hit forty, while women were over the hill. There were simply too many good veteran singers who got nothing but a snub from major record labels. This bothered Pam a lot.

By and large Pam also felt slighted because female acts were largely still viewed as opening acts. It didn't make a great deal of difference how hot you were, in order to sell the show, bookers always wanted to put a man on stage as the closer.

So even though Pam was playing country music's traditional meccas, like the Wheeling, West Virginia, Jamboree for as much as $16.75 a ticket, and selling out houses, she was still concerned that her ticket to ride was not going to be valid for long. The best way to insure a long trip was therefore to put together a new album that would cause everyone to realize that she was growing, not peaking. When she went into the studio, she came armed with the best material in town. Not only had she written a great deal of it, but she had chosen everything.

Arista had long ago figured out that they had signed an

artist with extraordinary drive and determination. Pam was determined to be the best she could be at everything. Ben could see his mom working to be the best mother. Bob saw how hard she worked at being a great mate. And those in the studio were amazed at just how much she gave in order to create the perfect album. Few people did this much when they were struggling, but to push this hard when you were hot was unheard of. Yet that is how much Pam wanted to stay around for a while.

As Pam laid down the tracks for the new album, she emphasized the importance of each cut. They were all her children and they all had a story to tell. If the message didn't get through, then a part of the perfection she was seeking was lost. She wanted the musicians to feel these cuts as much as she did.

Maybe the best of the best on this effort was a song that had been all but lost in Pam's past work. It was an old concept whose time had finally come.

"This idea was lifted out of another song I wrote," Pam remembered. "The song was originally 'All By My Lonesome,' and the line was 'No use crying over spilled perfume.' " It hit Pam that this wasn't a line, it was a title . . . a hook. "I was going through old tapes listening to the other song and it occurred to me that the phrase was a whole other story or song in itself."

That is where Dean Dillon entered the story. Dillon had come to Nashville with forty dollars in his pocket two decades before. He had recorded for a while, dated Tanya Tucker, lost both Tanya and his recording contract, and had kept himself going through his songwriting skills. Dean had scribed hits by George Strait such as "Unwound," "Marina Del Rey," "Ocean Front Property," "Nobody in His Right Mind," "It Ain't Cool to Be Crazy About You," "Holding My Own," and "I've Come to Expect It from You." Pam had met the songwriter and expressed an interest in working with him. From there, the two had set a meeting. Tillis couldn't wait to get started.

"I'm so glad Dean Dillon helped me with this," she told the press upon the album's release. "He's written so many great ballads for George Strait and others. He seemed like someone sensitive enough to tackle this subject with me."

Dean probably had no idea what Pam saw in him to write a woman's song. By and large, he was known for his "guy" songs. Yet he liked it that Pam was more than willing to give the team a chance. As each quickly discovered, Dillon and Tillis represented two opposite personalities. He worked quickly and was laid back. She took her time and crossed all the "t's" and dotted all the "i's." He was haphazard, she was detail oriented.

Pam remembered explaining "Spilled Perfume" 's story line to Dean. "I had to get him to think about it. That it was both about love and the recurring theme of friendship. I must have had those kinds of conversations a million times on the phone over the years. It seemed like something I needed to put to music and share with everyone who's ever been on either side of the situation."

During their first session in October, the songwriters put together a rough. A second session was set up to finish it off. That took just a little work. Then when it was recorded, Pam reworked the bridge again before finishing it off.

Dillon would say, "Each line was as good as we could get it, there's nothing weak." Given time, almost everyone else would agree.

Another song that Pam knew had to be a part of the album was "Mi Vida Loca," written by Pam and Jess Leary. Even before she went into the studio, she was using "Mi Vida Loca" to kick off her stage shows. It was getting a great response.

"I'll tell you just like I tell it onstage," Pam explained. "I got the idea for this one while channel surfing. I caught a piece of a Geraldo Rivera show about girl gangs. One very tough young lady had a tattoo that said, 'Mi Vida Loca.' Geraldo asked her about it, and she said, 'It's Spanish for, my crazy life. While I have no intention of getting a tattoo anytime soon, I know a good title when I hear one. These Spanish words, like so much of that language, have a beautiful ring. It presented a bit of a challenge for me since I don't speak a bit of Spanish, but Jess Leary and I worked it out to our satisfaction. Audiences everywhere have been really receptive to this Tex-Mex sound, especially when I explain what the title means. Most people can really relate to a 'crazy life.' "

Certainly Pam had known a life that was far from normal and bordered on crazy. What could be more crazy than trying to make a living in country music? If there was something, Pam hadn't found it yet.

Maybe the next most important song that the ensemble tackled during the session had been written by Doug Gill. It was so good that the album would use it as its title. In Pam's mind there was nothing quite like "Sweetheart's Dance."

"I just loved this song when I first heard it," she told Arista's public relations department. "It sounds like a cross between Sonny Curtis and Desert Rose. After all, John Jorgensen, from The Desert Rose Band did play guitar on this cut. Other than that, I don't know how you would classify it. It doesn't sound like anything else I've heard in a while. I just wanted to record something that makes people smile. I really like the irony in the line, 'Sometimes, babe, I hate you 'cause my love is so strong.' This is an intense relationship! But, these people are trying to keep their sense of humor and take life as it comes. Have fun; what a concept—'We make each other crazy, babe, and dance the Sweetheart's Dance' . . . makes sense to me."

" 'Til All the Lonely" had been written by Pam, her husband Bob DiPiero, and John Scott Sherrill. While the writing is top shelf, it was the way that Pam put it together in the studio that made this song special. After talking so much in the press about some of the oldtimers not getting a chance anymore, she gave a couple of very special ones another shot in the studio.

"This is the first song Bob, John Scott Sherrill, and I ever wrote together," Pam recalled. "At least the first draft was. I even tried to record the original version on the last album. It didn't make it—it wasn't ready to be born yet."

This statement gives a deep insight into just how deeply Pam feels about songwriting. Each one of her songs is a child. To fully get to its potential, it must grow and be given time to mature. " 'Til All the Lonely" took a bit longer than most of her songs.

"I was on a plane," Pam continued, "actually writing the liner notes for the last album when the story hit me right out of the blue. I wrote all the new verses in a flash of inspiration. I think it's a lot more unusual and interesting."

Then, as she thought about how to record it, Pam came up with something that really set this tune apart. "I always wanted my family to sing on it, but to be able to get all of them in the same place at the same time to do it was nothing short of miraculous. As they say in the old song [sort of], Daddy sang bass, sister sang tenor [Carrie, Connie, and Cindy], and me and little brother [Mel, Jr.] joined right in there. To top this hillbilly tour de force off, the legendary Bill Monroe played mandolin on it. I'm awfully proud of this one."

Pam later told Alan Sculley, "I don't care [if no one likes this one] if for no other reason than to do it for our family. It means the world to me, and I hope everybody will like it."

Then Pam stopped and added a special thought about Bill Monroe. "He was so gracious. I don't know how many country fans are also bluegrass fans, but it was just a thrill to get him there."

As Pam continued to build her album, she felt the weight of wondering if she could create the same magic that she had with her first two Arista releases. What if all this hard work was for nothing? Was bringing all these different kinds and influences of country music together really worth the price?

"There's always more pressure with every album," she would later admit. "The little higher you go, the pressure only increases. The good news is after a couple of albums, I feel pretty good. I feel a little bit of confidence. . . . I feel like I have a pretty good handle on what makes a good song."

Those in the studio agreed as she told them the story of each of the album's cut. With each side, things just seemed to get better. It was one of those rare occasions when the studio players weren't looking at their watches or getting bored. Pam had pulled out the stops and they were caught up in the same excitement that she felt. They sensed that this was quality stuff, not just a couple of good tunes and a lot of filler.

Pam had long been a fan of Dolly Parton. She liked her style and admired her guts. "Calico Plains" by Matraca Berg and Mike Nobel reminded her of Dolly. That was one of the big reasons she chose it for the album.

"I guess one of the things that drew me to this song is that it's about friendship—two women who grew up together and how their lives took different turns. Personally speaking, I have friends who have seen me go through a lot of romantic relationships, kids, marriage, and they've been a constant—your friends help keep you together through life's changes. So I relate to those women who value staying in touch. Musically, it's an acoustic moody sound, a little like 'Melancholy Child.' This song had a Dolly feel to it." And how she liked that!

Pam went back into the roots of rock to pull "When You Walk in the Room." Written by Jackie De Shannon, the singer/songwriter who was still remembered by almost every baby boomer for her "Son of a Preacher Man," this cut allowed Pam to invite a friendly rival to join her in the studio.

"Karla Bonoff covered this ['When You Walk in the

Room'] in the 70s,'' Tillis recalled when she had first heard it. At the time Pam hadn't known that it had been a De Shannon original. ''When Mary Chapin Carpenter came into the studio to sing on it, she told me she used to do it in her show. This is reaffirming that two fabulous songwriters see the magic in this very simple song just like I did. My coproducer, Steve Fishell, suggested this one, for which I'm eternally grateful. I love the big, acoustic 12-string sound.''

One of the reasons Pam loved that guitar was that her husband had been picking it. Another reason may have been that the 12-string sound was big in rock music during her formative years. And she still loved the rock music of her youth.

One of the other cuts on the album was ''Blown Away'' by Layng Martine, Jr. Pam liked it because it had a talk feel and she felt her fans would get a kick out of the message.

''This song is another one that I think is a lot of fun,'' she admitted. ''I like conversational lyrics. It's the anatomy of a crush; she sees this guy here and there and has it real bad for him. The next thing you know, he's on her front door step. I dedicate this to 'the young and in lust.' ''

At one time or another, everyone had been young and had coveted another. Pam could even see this one as a single.

''They Don't Break 'Em Like They Used To'' by Roger Brown and Jason Sellers pushed Pam a bit. Here was a song that had a cute title, one that might have come out of producer Tom Collins's warehouse and been cut by the likes of Sylvia. Yet there was more to this song than a hook, and Pam picked up on that in a hurry. She seemed to think her fans would too! Besides, it reminded her a bit of her father's kind of music.

''I'm a sucker for two things: a good play on words and a great country shuffle that people can wear out the dance floor on. I've got one on every album. This one is written by Roger Brown and Jason Sellers, a young kid from Texas, where they know about boot scootin'. Jason told me, 'Pam, the guys do fantastic with these kind of records. I don't know why more women don't record this kind of country.' I don't know either, but I'm happy to do my part. I'm even happier to have Vince Gill singing harmony like only Vince Gill can . . . he's perfection on two legs!''

Vince was now one of Nashville's top acts even though he had almost as much trouble landing a gig as Pam. Everyone had liked him and talked about his potential, but he had constantly been ignored by the fans. Then, thanks in no small part to the same man who helped Pam get noticed, Tim DuBois, Gill got his break. Yet even as hot and busy as he was, he was more than glad to come back in and join an old friend on the record.

The last two cuts on *Sweetheart's Dance* were equally special to the artist, but for two very different reasons. ''In Between Dances'' by Craig Bickhardt and Barry Alfonso was a song that Pam thought was just too beautiful not to grab. And ''Better Off Blue'' by Susan Longacre and Walt Aldridge, gave Tillis a chance to record again with her old Bluebird Cafe friends.

''Vicki Hampton and Ashley Cleveland, who sang on 'Maybe It Was Memphis,' are here again for some gutsy backgrounds on a rockin' track,'' Pam explained to the media upon the album's release. ''Then, I added Leanna Mavis, whose voice is higher to blend with me on the chorus. It's a lot of voices, a big sound. John Jorgensen did some more hot guitar work; this reminds me of some of my favorite old Linda Ronstadt records . . . simple and to the point.'' So, Pam was getting to rock out, and in Nashville, too!

Susan Longacre, ''Better Off Blue'' 's cowriter, had recently been an important part of Reba's career, too. She had been one of the writers of ''Is There Life Out There?'' So this kind of star treatment wasn't too bad either. The folks at Arista were hoping that some of the success would rub off. They wouldn't have to wait long to discover that it had!

Alanna Nash had long been one of the most respected voices in Nashville. When Ms. Nash listened to a preview of Pam's *Sweetheart's Dance,* she wrote, "Tillis has now placed herself among country's most accomplished modern women. That she can strike this kind of synthesis, both musical and personal, suggests that Tillis, like her father, is in it for the long haul." From the lady who had written the definitive biography of Dolly Parton, this was high praise, and Pam could only hope that Alanna was right and that all the hard work had paid off and this would be a long ride. As she waited for more judgments, Tillis kept her fingers crossed. At least she knew that even if the release was panned by the remainder of the critics, Nash had loved it. That counted for a great deal!

New Country loved it too. They stated in their five-star review, " 'Sweetheart's Dance' will have you pulling out your favorite albums to see if maybe, just maybe, this is the best country album by a woman in the '90s." The best in the decade? Yes, the work had been worth it!

Now realizing that they had goofed badly when they had mishandled Pam, Warner Brothers records released an album of her old cuts. They were hoping to make some "bunny money" off the new hot Pam. What they really did was reveal their own shortcomings.

Alanna Nash listened to the newly released old material for *Entertainment Weekly*. After studying the cuts, she wrote, "What a difference a new producer makes! Warner Brothers spent five years of the '80s trying to do what Arista then did in one, which is make Mel's little girl a star. Here's the best of what she recorded before leaving for her current label, including the first renditions of 'Maybe It Was Memphis' and 'One of Those Things.' The missing ingredients? Tillis's plucky personality and the supercharged vocals that now punch their way out of the radio."

New Country's review gave the *Pam Tillis Collection* three stars, two less than Pam's *Sweetheart's Dance.* This seemed to state the obvious.

So maybe Warner hadn't been wrong or even released the wrong material. Maybe they just didn't know how to do it. Maybe they didn't have the talent in house to give Pam the freedom to become a country music star. Or maybe the timing just wasn't right. One thing was for sure, Pam might have been the coyote in a dismal race with the road-runner a few years ago at Warner, but at Arista, the bird didn't stand a chance.

With another hit album under her belt, Pam hit the road again. Her shows with Alan Jackson were truly the summer's biggest hits. Yet with all her fine record releases, she was now running into a bit of a problem. Pam found herself having to drop some of her best songs when she opened for Jackson. There simply wasn't enough time. The forty-five minutes sets didn't allow her to feature everything and the new stuff too. Confident enough now to yell out "Do you know who my dad is?" Pam had now become a star who knew few peers. It was something she relished, but quietly.

Pam could really sense that she had arrived when she was asked to showcase her wares at New York's Bottom Line. She got this gig simply because of the advance review of *Sweetheart's Dance.* As Pam rocked, bookers and buyers were impressed and many went home feeling that they were seeing the next really hot female act. The phones lit up and bookers demanded the new star. It was attention that was long overdue for the "overnight" sensation.

What those in attendance at all of her shows, as well as most in Music City, didn't realize was that Pam wanted more than to be just the next great girl singer. Tillis knew that Reba had surpassed that identification. McEntire was a star and had all the power she needed to completely plot her own course. That is what Pam wanted too. And she had a plan for her next album that might just put her there, too.

Unlike so many others who exiled themselves from reality when fame came calling, success hadn't changed Pam; it just put more demands on her time. She ate the same, talked the same, and worked just as hard. She rarely cancelled shows because of illness, and kept telling everyone around her to remember how fame is at best fleeting. Her feet were anchored to the ground, and this may have just kept her career flying, too! Yet it was her focus on becoming something more than a star that really kept her motivated.

Meanwhile, she wasn't the only one in the family who was hot. Husband Bob DiPiero was coming on strong as a songwriter, too. Over the years, folks like Reba, Kathy Mattea, Marty Stuart, and Neal McCoy had all cut his songs. Bob had emerged as a presence in his own right. He was not just Pam's husband. He had an identity. The timing couldn't have been better for the marriage or for the man, because Bob's wife was about to make another huge jump up the ladder to superstardom.

It was no surprise when Pam was nominated for the Country Music Association's "Female Vocalist of the Year," for 1994. She had earned this nomination because of her sales and body of work. Yet many figured that she wouldn't win the honor. Tillis's friend Mary Chapin Carpenter had won it two years running. A host of other talents were in place this year, too. And Reba was there. It seemed to most like Reba was always there.

Surprisingly, Reba had not won this award since 1987, but for some reason, the public seemed to think she had won it every year for a decade. As Pam looked at this fact, she knew that Reba's was the kind of success she wanted for her own career. Reba didn't need awards or honors, she simply got by on talent and drive. She was so big that nothing could stop her. She was so powerful that she simply couldn't be challenged. Even when she lost, she won. And McEntire couldn't be categorized because within the parameters of a very well-planned rise to the top, she had taken chances, too. She had even sung a soul song during the awards show. She had demanded "R-E-S-P-E-C-T," and she had gotten it.

In a sense, Pam had already met Reba in that area. And the knowledge that Tillis had had such success despite the fact that she couldn't be categorized into only one niche of country music had come to mean a great deal to her. She didn't fit a mold and her sound embraced so many themes and influences that even her fans couldn't find anyone to whom to compare her. Of course, when it came to voting, this could work also against her. The folks who won the awards usually were people whom others could peg. Those who were betting were not dwelling on Pam's chances.

So it shocked many, including Pam, when Tillis won the CMA "Female Vocalist of the Year." On stage she beamed and said, "*I love this town*!" It was a love that had been hard earned. For years, Music City found her a bit too strange to deal with. Now the community, which still didn't really know what to make of her, was finding out that she was bit too talented to ignore and finally rewarding her for her years of "dogged determination."

While folks like Connie Smith, Marty Stuart, and others were overjoyed for Mel's daughter, the critics were thrilled, too. The writers knew that country music now had a new and powerful voice who wasn't trying to be the next Reba clone. She didn't sound like anyone else. She wasn't old country or new country. She was simply Pam. She was daring, but she was accessible. She had humor, but she took her work seriously.

In an after-show press conference, Pam simply and modestly stated that the award gave her "credibility." Yet she didn't feel like winning had given her real stardom or lifetime security. She even hinted that the toughest times were ahead.

"Show business is one business where you have to prove yourself over and over again," she had explained. "Getting the chance is tough."

Barbara Fairchild and Mel would have loved to have the opportunity to prove themselves to the whole spectrum of country music again. Yet the doors weren't opcn to these past winners anymore. How long would they be open for Pam? Would she just become the last pretender rather the next contender? Only time would tell.

Chapter Twelve

The 1994 Country Music Association's "Female Vocalist of the Year" didn't waste much time resting on her honor. While most stars might have taken a few weeks off, done some shopping or hit a hot vacation spot, Pam Tillis went back to work. She was bound and determined to do something that no country music woman, not even Reba, had ever done. It was time for a revolution in country music. And who better to light the fuse and start it than a former rebel rocker?

Tillis gave hints as to wanting to do something explosive when she told CMA *Close Up*, "There's another level I'll be aspiring to . . . I really want to try and make some fans out there. This is coming from a person who spent a lot of time on the flip side of this. I got to be artistic for years and years (without commercial success)." Now Pam had something else in mind.

Pam considered all of her years of practically starving to death for her art and added, "Been there, done that." But those who read between the lines in *Close Up* must have wondered just what it was that Mel's daughter was up to now.

With the power of winning the major award in her pocket, and sales going through the roof on her latest effort, it appeared to many that Pam already had a slew of fans and some pretty major commercial success, so what was she really intimating to the CMA magazine? Or was the singer/songwriter hinting at something that would add another title to her impressive professional handle? Although she hadn't told too many people, what she really wanted was to produce. In Music City, this was unheard of. Yet Pam felt it was something she had "grown" into and the time had arrived. Still, as strongly as Pam felt this, she hedged her bets when she finally began to speak of producing.

"It's not calculated at all," claimed the girl who once slept in her father's guitar case during recording sessions. "Things come to you at a certain time, and you take what comes to you with the faith that it's right. You can't always ask 'why' about everything.

"I've participated heavily in everything I've done. Producing is what I needed to do this time. This is the way I felt I could grow the most. I didn't go into production thinking that I knew everything there was to know, I was willing to experiment and learn along the way. The reason for producing is just to maintain a stamp of individuality; and to identify, once and for all, where my own strengths and weaknesses in the studio are."

Producing an album did represent another stage in growth for Pam. And personally it was an important one, too! As someone who was frightened to death of stagnation, this was a way to ensure that she was moving herself and her career in the right direction. Besides, this move also signalled a continuation of what she had made an effort to do for some time. As she herself had noted, over the past few years, Pam had become involved in every aspect of her career. She made the business decisions with her manager Mike Robinson. She didn't let him act alone. She had long decided what happened on her road shows and had also taken over approving package dates. She picked out or wrote her own songs and hired her band. She even set lights and sound if she felt they weren't right. She was a take-charge woman, always had been, and, given the opportunity, always would be.

Yet producing an album would represent a first for a country music woman. No one, certainly not Dolly, Reba, or even Barbara Mandrell or Loretta Lynn, had ever attempted it. A generation before, when Patsy Cline was the first big ''girl'' singer, no one would have even dared whisper it. And maybe in many ways that was good. Cline consistently hated songs which legendary producer Owen Bradley played for her, many of which, such as ''Crazy'' and ''I Fall to Pieces,'' were to become her signature numbers. Who is to say if the women who came before Pam really knew and understood what a producer had to do? Who really knows if they could have separated themselves from their identity as an artist? Could they have kept their fingers on the consumer's pulse while also satisfying their own artistic urges? For that matter could Pam? This had to be a question she was even asking herself.

''That's [production] the last boys' club in country music, but this is the decade that it is going to change,'' Robert K. Oermann, author of *Finding Her Voice: The Saga of Women in Country Music,* told *Country Weekly.* He just hadn't guessed how soon.

Even though she was about to set the music world buzzing, Pam seemed oblivious to the trail she was blazing. To her, it just seemed like the time to expand the scope of what she was doing. It was time to push the envelope and grow. She was searching for all the potential she had, a search that had consumed a great deal of her life. This was another in a series of experiments. Surprisingly, no one at Arista stood in the way of her grab for production power.

One of the reasons so many Arista executives stood by and let Tillis plot her own course is that she had a much better feel for herself that any other star in their stable. It may have come from growing up around the business, or having had a career that had had so many false starts, or maybe even a combination of both, but she seemed to know her own strengths and weaknesses. She always seemed to know what she could and couldn't do. There were no false images, Pam always saw herself as she really was. And this knowledge and her own self-confidence in her sound allowed her to surround herself with talented people who were not afraid to speak their minds, too. In other words, Pam did not surrounded herself with "yes" folks. She knew the only way to grow was to listen and apply what others thought and believed, too. So in spite of the fact that Tillis might have been on the edge in some of her tastes and concepts, the record label and Tim Dubois also knew that this "go-for-it attitude" would be tempered by the reality of the marketplace.

When Pam approached Tim about taking over production of the next album, he simply said, "Sure." To her mentor and Arista's CEO, it was not a problem. With the success she had already given him and the company, DuBois would have probably even let her produce a few other acts, too. With the new title, the singer/songwriter/producer went to work on putting together the best album Nashville had ever seen. And she was prepared. Still, an interview with *New Country*'s Brian Mansfield indicated that she thought she might have had to put up a bit more of a fight to get the rights to produce. She sounded surprised that there were no protests.

"They [Arista and Tim DuBois] didn't bat an eye. It was just a non-issue. They're either letting me start a new career or they've giving me enough rope to hang myself."

Arista and Pam seemed to realize that she wasn't going to commit career suicide. Part of this thinking had to come with just how closely Pam had noted every single she had ever released and the reason it had been a success or a flop. She simply wasn't a singer who didn't keep tabs on her career. She seemed to know more than anyone. This was a producer's job and Pam was already doing it! Why not let her get paid for it?

This kind of career-intensive thinking seemed to be revealed when she told Alan Sculley of *Music Monthly,* "Every single I've released has been a little bit different than the last. And that's been really fun for me because I get bored easily. I've never wanted to be typecast, and so I find this era in country music to be a perfect spot for a person like me." Not wanting to get bored also seemed to indicate a producer's mentality to stay on the edge of what was happening at the moment, not rely on past successes.

In fact, Pam sensed that the audience was picking up on her evolution and liking it too. Yet as much as she picked up on how the change was working for her, she also knew that she couldn't tinker with the product too much, too fast. Radio was the key to getting the message out, and the stations weren't going to get too radical all at once. So she had to keep the releases commercial. For Pam, this kind of realization represented the growth that gave Arista the ultimate confidence to turn her loose.

As Pam faced the newest and biggest challenge of her career, she admitted to a bit of apprehension. Yet she also felt that she was ready. She told those working with her, "I'm starting to trust my instincts a little bit. And there's also something comforting in the fact of knowing that you're doing everything you can do to make it turn out good. It's not like, oh God, I didn't have time to be there. I'll never forgive myself. Or I didn't take enough time in picking the songs, or I wasn't in the mood when I sang that vocal. When you do everything you can do and give your very best, then no matter what happens, you have the comfort of knowing that. And that's where it's at." You also don't have anyone else to blame.

With that philosophy she charged on and began looking for songs. Surprisingly, she didn't look at home this time as much as she had in the past. Unlike most male stars who had turned producer, she backed away a bit from her own inspiration. Some of those in the studio were shocked that as gifted a storyteller as Pam would do this. Yet, seemingly like everything else since her arrival at Arista, Tillis had a reason for looking at other songwriters' stuff first.

"I thought outside songs would help me have a broader voice and express some attitudes that might not come from my pen," the producer explained. This search could also have something to do with wearing the producer's hat. Pam added, "There was an objectivity as a producer with the outside material that I might not have been able to have with my own stuff."

Pam constantly pointed out that this move would allow her to eliminate a problem that she saw in the current production system, too. "In Nashville," the singer explained, "producers work with multiple acts, and that kind of replication scares me. Not that they don't make fine records, but I wanted to stay away from that machine because I'm more of an individual maverick soul. I'd rather go down my own little path like I've always done, and it's just me, now, so there are no filters."

Tillis, the producer, worked from November 22 to January 25 putting together the seamless sound that is so important for her. Steve Fishell, her coproducer, has rarely seen an artist work that hard and long, many times putting in sixteen- and eighteen-hour days. She had even given up quality time at home, which was something Tillis rarely did. This was how important she considered this assignment. She was simply not going to waste the chance at production. It had to be more than a one-time venture. Once again, Pam seemed to be out to win the respect of the Music City community.

No doubt many in the industry were a bit doubtful that Mel's daughter could handle a chore this large. There was a great deal more to getting the perfect sound and material together than most artists realized. Besides, by and large, performers were simply not detailed-oriented people. They left the organizational stuff to the managers and band leaders. They just wanted to sing, smile, and go back to the bus. It was hard for music veterans to picture Pam having the kind of drive and clear head it took to do as well on this project as a seasoned professional. Once again, many were predicting that Tillis would fail and that her label would regret giving her this much power. Of course, the Nashville establishment had been wrong before!

The folks who turned out to work with her felt differently. When Pam gathered the musicians in the studio, it was like old-home week.

"I've worked with many of them [studio musicians] since I was a kid," explained Tillis about the security she felt in the studio. "I've never gotten anything but support from the musicians here. So it was really gratifying to be in the studio by myself and feel that coming from those people."

The humor that had been so much a part of Pam's life and so evident in her shows and past recording was what most musicians expected to see when they got a look at the numbers she had chosen. Yet that was not the sound that Pam had in mind. The material was more serious in tone than her past mix. With the power in her hands, she seemed bent on doing exactly what she had told the press women needed to do in country music—provide a message of song for the women who needed a voice. So maybe for that reason, the songs as well as the production seemed as finely drawn as a well-written novel.

"The sound is organic," Tillis explained as she went to work, "I'm drawn to that kind of purity, but the record is not sparsely produced. It's layered; there are a lot of things going on. I'm really anxious, as usual, to see how it's received."

Pam chose "All of This Love," as the album's title cut. Certainly with the time and devotion that Tillis was using to craft this project, there was a lot of love involved in each track. So maybe this song was appropriate.

"All of This Love" had been written by John Paul Daniel, Chapin Hartford, and Jule Medders, and Pam had liked it from the beginning. Of the hundreds of demos she screened, this one really jumped out. Besides, the tune had an inside track—Chapin Hartford had written one of Pam's first big hits, "Shake the Sugar Tree".

"The thing I like about Chapin Hartford is that she can hit the nail on the head in such an original way," Pam informed the press upon the album's release. "There's something really pretty and folksy about a beginning: 'Have you ever seen a wild magnolia?' It sounds like something Dolly Parton would sing. What better reason could there be to record it?"

Once again Pam's infatuation with Dolly's sound came into play when choosing one of the most important cuts for an album. But why not find something that Parton would cling to? Both Dolly and Pam had wonderful soprano voices and both performers loved songs that were wrapped in layers of story-telling fabric.

Next Pam chose "Deep Down," a new cut by Walt Aldridge and John Jarrad because it was "a hard-hitting song with a 'to the bone' lyric that doesn't mince words. But it's set against a deceptively bouncy melody which, for some reason, reminds me of Sonny Curtis in the chorus."

Yet unlike many of the other cuts on the album, Pam hadn't discovered this one on her own. As she explained, "Deep Down" came from higher up.

"A funny thing happened in a meeting with Tim DuBois. He said, 'Can I play you something?' I thought he wanted my opinion on it for another artist, because he always tells me he trusts my ears. He played me that song, and I thought, 'Why doesn't anybody every pitch me something like this? That sounds like a hit!' When it was over, he said, 'Well what do you think?' and I said, 'I love it—who's it for?' He said, 'You!' "

Most artists who just record music and go home don't consider the meaning and impact of each song. They don't study it. They don't let it grow on them and consider what it will mean to their lives. Most artists take their material for granted. By and large, it is like a meal that has been prepared for them by someone else and all that they have to do is consume it and go home. Yet for Pam each song on each album has a special meaning and reason for being. Such was the case for a Bruce and John Hornsby original called "Mandolin Rain."

"I felt that it would be nice to have a literal treatment of this song," Pam recalled about her production instructions. "I'm really proud of the arrangement and I feel like we pulled off making it unique to me. We wrestled with it; in fact, there were some tense moments. Some things are just simple to map out, but this wasn't. All the musicians worked really hard. You look for things that work for you as an artist. 'Mandolin Rain,' to me, is very reminiscent of 'Maybe It Was Memphis.' "

Imagery was something that Pam seemed to seek in almost every tune she chose for this project. Yet that was hardly surprising as Tillis had long been involved in defining the moments of her own life through music. Going back to even before her days of singing "I Don't Know How to Love Him," in *Jesus Christ Superstar*, Pam knew the impact of words arranged in a poetic manner. That is probably why she reached for Angelo and Kim Richey's country-feeling "Sunset Red."

"The thing I liked about this song is that it's really two songs in one. It has a very atmospheric verse, and then a really straight-ahead country chorus. It's very visual, and I like visual songs. Being a fan of Kim Richey, I had been wanting to cut one of her songs for a while. I was waiting for the perfect fit; and this is it."

Tillis the producer probably couldn't wait to get her hands on a piece by master tunesmith Don Schlitz, but she had no idea just what Don and Gerry House had composed until she listened to the demo of "The River and the Highway." It not only moved her emotionally, but it moved her to enlarge her production plans, too!

"I cried the first time I heard this song, and I wasn't even feeling particularly sensitive that day. We called the publisher to put it on hold for the album and, coincidentally, Tim DuBois had just put it on hold for me. The idea I had for the arrangement was kind of scary—my first outing as a producer and I'm going in asking my label for a budget to record strings.'' Needless to say, Tim came through with the violins.

''You Can't Have a Good Time Without Me'' by Lewis Anderson, Lisa Silver, and Russell Smith probably sounded as much like the Pam that most people knew as any of the album's cuts. As Pam would explain, ''This song is really cute and tongue-in-cheek. For some reason, I'm fascinated by the comic potential of self-delusion. It was nice to have it to lighten up the album. It allowed me to use a little bit of my jazz experience in a western swing context. I think this is one of my best vocals on the album.''

Of course, by combining jazz and western swing she had merged two musical influences that were important to the early days of her career and her father's. Mel had spent a bit of time singing lead for Bob Wills and His Texas Playboys. Wills, the King of Western Swing, had long considered himself more of a jazz musician than a country act, and Bob had brought the freedom of jazz to his type of dance sound. Pam had also spent some time with jazz during her free-form days in San Francisco. ''You Can't Have a Good Time Without Me'' simply tied a few of the Tillis family's loose ends together.

Probably the most unique choice that Pam made was ''Betty's Got a Bass Boat.'' Many wondered if anyone would ever record the whimsical piece by Bernie Nelson and Craig Wiseman. Yet when Pam heard it, she liked it, perhaps because of her own love of fishing. And when she heard the story behind it, she loved the song.

''This is a true story,'' Tillis explained. ''One of the guys who wrote it went to a little catfish restaurant out in a small southern town. While he was sitting there eating, this really odd couple walked in: a very handsome man and a kind of ordinary woman. So he started wondering, 'How did these two get together?' Then they walked out; and she hopped up in the driver's seat of this big truck hitched to a new bass boat! So he called his cowriter, who was on his honeymoon, and left a message on his answering machine. The cowriter called back and said, 'If you write that with anybody else before I get back, I will kill you!'

"What can I say? Here is someone with the right kind of ammunition in the war of the sexes!" One has to wonder if this will start a new trend for women looking to pick up men. And if this lure works, will they give Pam the credit?

Pam had long loved the work of Kim Carnes, so it was little wonder that she found a place in her set for "No Two Ways About It." The cut was written by Carnes, Greg Barnhill, and Vince Melamed.

"Just as I won't shy away from something on the edge like 'Betty's Got a Bass Boat,' I won't shy away from something this strong. It's an unabashedly sad song—the flip side of good times. It's someone saying, 'This is the way it is,' and there's a certain strength in reaching that point. I've been through heartbreak, so I feel qualified to sing about it. There are people out there going through it; and hearing this kind of song can be cathartic. I'm looking forward to putting it in my show. I have a feeling that it will go over very well in concert."

Pam was always bent on reaching emotions with her music. She wanted to bring up smiles, but also tears. She wanted people to see their lives in her work. That is the reason she felt so strongly about giving so much. That is also why she looked so hard and long for the songs she placed in front of the session players. Though she seemed to be reaching a long way for most of the cuts, Pam didn't have to go far for the final two songs. The first had been written by Pam and her brother Mel Tillis, Jr. Pam quickly realized that it was a winner because she had already tried the Tex-Mex ballad out in her live shows and it had gotten great response. So there was no question that "Tequila

Mockingbird'' had a home in the ''All of This Love'' package.

''I'm proud of this song; it's special because I wrote it with my brother. I've been performing it in my live show and a lot of people have come backstage after the show and mentioned that they really liked it after hearing it just one time.''

In order to give the song the feel that Pam wanted, she brought in a bluegrass master to sing along. She was a bit nervous when she began to show what she wanted to John Starling of Seldom Scene. But as she soon discovered, he had the bases covered.

''My goodness, what a bluegrass stylist!'' Pam exclaimed. ''This is hard to explain, but I was in the studio thinking, 'How would he sing?' [Soon] I was learning the song from him, even thought he had never heard it.''

The final cut really cut close to home. ''It's Lonely Out There'' was a husband and wife collaboration and one that the writers, Bob DiPiero and Pam Tillis, couldn't have done any better.

''Another title for this song could be 'Trust Me on This One.' '' Pam admitted. ''The given title came to me somehow while I was driving home one afternoon. I told Bob my idea and he asked, 'Well, do you hear it as an up-tempo, or a ballad?' By the time I could explain to him how I thought it should go, he'd pretty much written it while I was still figuring it out in my head. I have to fine tune a song in my brain before I write it down on paper. So, I took a nap and when I woke up, the first thing on my mind was the bridge on [Johnny Nash's 1972 hit] 'I Can See Clearly Now.' ''

Pam was quick to add, ''Mind you, we're not stealing; we're paying homage.''

Tillis the writer and Tillis the producer thought a great deal alike. They gave songs time to grow and spent a great deal of time nurturing them. This probably came from

Pam's belief that true inspiration came from the soul, not the brain.

Pam explained her thoughts like this: "A lot of times music will be forming on a subconscious level; and when you open your mouth and try to sing the very first line, you're further along than you think. They say the best ones are like that." If this project was any example of Pam's heart and soul, then they were something very special.

Everyone at Arista was thrilled with the final product. Pam was just thrilled with the chance to be a producer. Yet even after she had put the project to bed, she had her doubts if it was her best effort.

"I've been fortunate to work with good people," she observed as she considered the effort. "I still have to think in my mind and in my heart that I haven't done all I can do." There was nothing else to do, but go back on the road and play for the fans. And she was making a bunch of them, and more than a few were disc jockeys who just couldn't get enough of her stuff.

Austin, Texas, DJ Brad Hansen was one of her biggest pushers. He told *Billboard,* "Because there are so many good country acts coming out, I feel like Pam Tillis has been a little overlooked. I think she writes intelligent songs, and she doesn't settle for the easy hook or a formula."

Whatever it was that Pam was doing was obviously working. By the spring of 1995 *Sweetheart's Dance* had topped the charts for eight months, TNN had asked her to host a few hour-long specials from the old Opry House, and she had a line of interviews with the press that stretched on forever. Yet the singer wanted to take some time off. The killer work she had done producing her album and the road shows were taking their toll. She longed for the days of spare hours spent writing or fishing. She missed the time on a lake, listening to friends' stories, watching time drag by. She wanted and probably needed a chance to unwind and pull herself out of the pace that living on the road demanded. She wanted to again assume the role of the tomboy who liked to roam the woods looking for a simpler type of adventure. Of course, when she had had the time to pursue these idle time exploits, she had also been nearly starving to death.

Pam has just wrapped up an appearance with Jay Leno of *The Tonight Show* and was planning to spend a week at home with her son and husband. It was a time when she had vowed that nothing was going to get in the way of her family time. She had even refused all requests for bookings because Ben had a week off from school and she felt they needed some time together. She thought that nothing could interfere with this week or make her change her plans. How many times had Mel thought that when Pam was a child? Then David Letterman called. This was New York, the big time, and a chance to appeal to a new audience. She was also going to have a chance to work with Paul Schaffer and his band. So much for a full week off. So while Pam might have once told the press that she couldn't work like Reba, in reality, now she was. Even as she assumed more control over her career, that career was also taking more control of the rest of Pam's life.

In August 1995, Pam, Bob, and Ben moved into a new home in the woods outside of Nashville. Their new digs were not fancy, just a place to get away and think, create, and fish. When people wondered why she wasn't living like a star, Pam explained that she didn't go for more splendor because in her new home she had everything she needed in the trees, the critters, and the quiet nights. This was a place where she could communicate with not only her husband and son, but herself. And for Pam, with so much falling squarely on her shoulders, knowing herself was more important now than ever.

The new home was also a place to leave behind the trappings of stardom. Here she really could be a mom, a cook, a tomboy, and a friend. The demands she had in this woodsy world were seemingly smaller, but in a very real sense, much more important. Here she had the time to listen to her son's dreams and goals and to try to give him the time in his youth she had often missed because her own father worked so long and so much. She admitted to those who knew her well that her dream for Ben was for him to have something he really feels passionately about as she did music. She also hoped that he can take that passion and use it as a way to live his life, like she had with hers. Still, she didn't want her son to struggle as hard as she had.

The first single off the *All of This Love* album was released September 25, 1995. It was destined to be a hit. And so was the "Pam-produced" album. Any questions Music City doubters might have had about her ability to put out a first-class project were answered in the stellar reviews.

Alanna Nash, who was becoming one of Ms. Tillis's loudest supporters, wrote for *Entertainment Weekly,* "On her first outing as a solo producer, Tillis exercises her love of sinewy ballads ('The River and the Highway') and novelty tunes ('Betty's Got a Bass Boat'). This album is less serious than last year's breakthrough *Sweetheart's Dance,* which made her a major player. Less grabby too." But Nash still liked it!

Bruce Honick, writer for *Country Weekly,* wrote, "She's earned the respect of her peers as a result of sheer talent, years of hard work, and dogged determination."

Billboard chimed in by recognizing the full effects of Pam's efforts. The publication wrote, "Besides the finished product, Pam Tillis's career has been distinguished by her unusually high degree of involvement in all aspects of the recording process. On her new Arista album 'All of This Love,' set to be released November 7, Tillis has finally taken the ultimate step."

USA Today voices some of the highest praise for the new producer. "Pam Tillis's compelling voice, which has an odd instrumental quality, shows its many colors in her new 'All of This Love.' . . . Tillis dares to pour on the textures, even some heavy jazz overtones."

Closer to home, *The Tennessean,* which had raved about

her since her days in *Superstar,* gave the album high marks too. "It's a great one . . . [it] will bowl you over . . . 'Deep Downs' ' sawing fiddles pay a nod to the era in which Mel Tillis first came to Nashville, but the hand claps and a hint of rock guitar make it spunky." Yes, by almost everyone in every venue, Pam was now being recognized for where she came from and who she had become.

Maybe the proudest member of the team was Tim DuBois. "She's now standing free as a producer," Arista's head honcho bragged. "(She's) the first woman in quite a while who's produced her own album. But she's always had a tremendous amount of input on her albums. Just ask Steve Fishell or Paul Worley [former Tillis producers]. The great thing about Pam is that she's not just an entertainer, but an artist who knows who she is and what works for her and what doesn't. She not only writes a good portion of her albums, but she also finds a good portion of the rest. When she came to me about producing herself, the only thing that scared me was getting the paperwork done!"

With the reviews in and the sales beginning to take off, the record company now fully publicized the fact that Pam was the full-blown producer on the album. Arista took great pleasure in using this fact to set Tillis apart from every other woman in the business. As they like to say, "Even Reba hasn't produced!"

Arista quoted Pam as saying, "It [the new album] doesn't sound like cookie-cutter country. There's a kind of 'layered-up' sound. You hear something different every time, and I wrote only two songs—"Tequila Mockingbird" and "It's Lonely Out There," but what became interesting as the producer was that the music spoke through the musicians as an extension of me."

Tillis's statements seemed to indicate she felt a woman could do this job better than a man when she said, "The album tells you right off the bat where this is coming from. It's all dolled up in emotional intensity, unlike the last one, which was more fun-spirited and nice."

Finally Pam used Arista's platform to state what she had wanted people to understand about her for years. She was a combination of all the music genres she had listened to, not just one form.

"I am lucky that my style is a non-style," Pam told the media, "I feel like a recording equivalent of a character actress. I cast myself in different roles and don't get typecast, and people expect that of me. My material is always changing, and it changes with me. I'm just glad that an artist like me with all these feelings can make a career in country music."

The final statement may have been the most important. Yes, now country music was large enough for someone who refused to be just like everyone else. It was a place where Pam could really be at home and really do anything she wanted to try to do—even produce. She didn't say it, but those who watched her expected her to smile and proudly state for all women, "We've come a long way, baby." Certainly Pam had!

With all the good things that were happening now, most expected Tillis to win the CMA's "Female Vocalist of the Year" title again. Instead she gave up the crown to newcomer Alison Krauss. It was a bittersweet moment. Pam would have loved to have taken the award again. Certainly the year she had just experienced would have deemed it a justifiable reward. But it was good to see another hardworking individual get the honor. As Pam told *New Country,* "I had a good year and I'll win it back. I ain't goin' nowhere."

Not only wasn't she going anywhere, but it seemed like everyone wanted to work with her. Burt Bacharach, whose first hit was the country song "The Story of My Life," recorded by Marty Robbins in 1958, returned to Nashville. Initially his interest was piqued because he had scored a country hit with "On My Own," a vocal event number in which Trisha Yearwood, Martina McBride, and Linda Davis had joined superstar Reba McEntire on both the video and the single release. Yet Burt, who had a track record of pop hits including "One Less Bell to Answer," by the Fifth Dimension, Herb Alpert's "This Guy's in Love with You," Christopher Cross's "Arthur's Theme," B. J. Thomas's "Raindrops Keep Falling on My Head," Dionne Warwick's "I Say a Little Prayer," and "That's What Friends Are For," by Gladys Knight, Stevie Wonder, and a host of others, had really come to town to write new country-oriented songs. And one of those with whom he wanted to work was Pam Tillis. He wanted Pam simply because she was one of the best. The much awarded veteran writer thought he could learn a great deal about the new country sound from her. Now the singer/songwriter/producer whose favorite movie was *Thelma and Louise* was beginning to realize that she had even more fans and more power than she had dreamed. Hey, she was even more of a force than Thelma and Louise combined!

With that in mind, Pam now freely allowed her imagination to run wild with ways that she could shake up and freshen up the industry. She talked about filming an entire video with a hand-held camcorder. She was also thinking of using a new release for that concept, maybe one of her own songs, but not even appearing in the video herself.

"Why?" Mario Tarradell of the *Dallas Morning News* asked her when she explained the concept to him. He was probably having problems even conceiving of why anyone would want to make such a radical move. Pam's answer was predictable—if you knew Pam.

"You get locked into a format. There's got to be some other way to use this medium . . . You can't limit yourself."

That is what she didn't want to happen. She didn't want to fall into a comfortable shell and simply redo the old formula just because it worked. She wanted to really use her talent and power in ways to widen the scope of music that was out there, and at the same time give women a louder creative voice in Nashville. Yet when she began to think of doing something wild in a video format, she ran back into the conservative elements of the Nashville establishment, many of whom made the decisions at CMT and TNN. These were the same folks who had banned a Garth Brooks video that made a real statement about domestic violence. Martina McBride suffered the same fate when she had gone into that area. Statements were out. So, it seemed, was real creative storytelling such as Reba McEntire's "Is There Life Out There?" "Use the formula and do it like everyone else does it" was what they wanted.

"It is hard to be creative and daring in an atmosphere of caution," Pam roared back. "People that market country music tend to want to handle country audiences with kid gloves. I can't say it's unwarranted, but I do think it's a little heavy handed. Everybody is exposed to everything. I don't feel a country artist lives in a vacuum. But that is where my artistic intuition is at odds with the research."

Research or not, Pam was hot. She might have broken a few rules and stretched a few limits, but the girl who once couldn't give a rock album effort away was now the woman whom almost everyone else wanted to emulate. Since 1991, she had earned three gold albums. "Put Yourself in My Place" in 1991 had been the first. It was the record that really got her career kick-started. *Homeward Looking Angel* in 1992 had not only gone gold, but also platinum, and proven that she was not just a flash in the pan. *Sweetheart's Dance*, released in 1994 (also gold and platinum), was the record that had given her the power to produce her fourth album. This release was also destined to go gold and beyond. Few women outside of Reba and the hot new Canadian singer, Shania Twain, could claim sales like that. And Pam's were building, not subsiding. While Reba may have looking at the down side of the mountain, Pam seemed to be still heading up!

When few women, including McEntire, could get to the top of the single charts, Tillis had run the numbers for three number 1's. The trio—"Don't Tell Me What to Do,"

"When You Walk in The Room," and "Mi Vida Loca"—had become standards. And seven more of Pam's cuts had landed in the top ten. Those included "One of Those Things," "Put Yourself in My Place, "Maybe It Was Memphis," "Shake the Sugar Tree," "Cleopatra, Queen of Denial," "Do You Know Where Your Man Is?" and one of her personal favorites, "Spilled Perfume."

This long list of hits had no doubt earned her the CMA "Female Vocalist of the Year" award in 1994, and nominations the next year. And pulling down the honor had done more than legitimatize the singer/songwriter/producer. It had given her a forum to become more than Mel's daughter. She was a media darling!

In a brief two-year period she was the envy of other stars, as Pam had appeared on *The Late Show with David Letterman, The Tonight Show, CBS This Morning, Full Access: On Tour with Pam Tillis, Live at the Ryman with Pam Tillis, CNN's Showbiz Today, South Bank Show* (UK), and a long list of other marquee television shows. She had also experienced acting through a brief bit in *LA Law,* and in the tele-movie *XXX's and OOO's.*

In her spare time, of which she now had very little, Pam had even reviewed other artists' records for the publication *New Country.* And most importantly, she had produced. She was a five-foot, six-inch, one-hundred-and-twenty-pound, blue-eyed brunette who had come a long way since her days of struggling to find herself in San Francisco and in rock music. Yet her advice to newcomers, "Be unique, don't be a cookie cutter of someone else," sounded very much like the young woman who dropped out of college to find herself in jazz and rock. This seemed to prove that her life had changed, she had grown, but under it all, she was still the same person.

One of the biggest surprises of early 1996 came when Pam helped changed the entire pattern of how to book country music shows. Pam had long railed against the concept that it took a man to close a show. She thought that men weren't even needed to draw crowds in today's market. Yet her thoughts had largely been ignored, until now. With a bit of insight and a lot of faith, a large corporation decided to throw caution to the wind and follow Pam's advice.

The Kraft Country Tour announced that they would sponsor a country music showcase that featured singers Lorrie Morgan, Pam Tillis, and Carlene Carter as headliners in 1996. The 33-city tour, which would last from the last week of May 1996 to September 1996, thus became the first country music tour to be headlined by only women. Booking arrangements were coordinated by two giants, William Morris Agency and Buddy Lee Attractions. The tour was even planning video segments showing the family heritage of each act. A part of the proceeds would benefit the Second Harvest Food Bank and be used to feed homeless and hungry people all across the nation. In other words, this was a big deal, so big a deal that the announcement even ran on the AP wire and in *USA Today*.

Marty Stuart had long called the three women the "Opry Brats." This was a direct play on the ladies having grown up backstage while their parents worked the audience. Yet the fact that the trio was a part of country music history was not lost on Kraft. After all, Kraft had been sponsoring country music on television since the time when most video images were black and white. Because of this knowledge of the genre and its fans, Kraft didn't anticipate any trouble selling tickets for the all-female event. Robert Hopton, director of marketing for Kraft, confidently stated, "We were looking forward to doing something that hadn't been done before and also looking for heritage in country music. With the talent of these women on this stage, how could we go wrong?"

"It is unique and something that I've been wanting to do for awhile," Tony Conway of Buddy Lee Attractions chimed in. "It's also something the girls have been wanting to do."

At the press conference, Ms. Morgan added, "It is a wonderful day when three women in country music can pull off a tour."

Meanwhile Pam, who had probably given the movers and shakers the idea in the first place, simply sounded humble. "I feel Kraft is giving us the opportunity to make some wonderful memories on this tour." And a lot of money too!

The Opry Brats were booked into every major city in the United States on a coast-to-coast tour that would rival the itinerary of any top rock group. They had been guaranteed the finest production that money could buy. They were assured that while it was their show to work, the sky was still the limit. They could do what they wanted as long as the fans approved. With long lines of men and women lining up for tickets, it was no doubt that this event would start a trend.

If the tour wasn't enough to make Pam beam, then being nominated for a Grammy had to light up her eyes. The five female country nominees were Alison Krauss, "Baby Now That I've Found You"; Patty Loveless, "You Don't Even Know Who I Am"; Martina McBride, "Safe in the Arms of Love"; Shania Twain, "Any Man of Mine"; and Pam's "Mi Vida Loca (My Crazy Life)." Pam didn't win. That honor once again fell to Krauss. Yet Tillis was in the big time, and that was all that mattered.

Vince Gill, who had once struggled alongside Tillis summed up what made this thirty-nine-year-old woman special. In *Country Weekly*, Vince observed, "Every time she sings a new song, you know you're listening to a lady who wants to do it all—and probably will."

For Pam, who had spent so much time just working to be recognized as something other than her father's daughter, the irony of suddenly being one of the hottest ten acts in country music did not escape her. It also didn't cause her to lose her grip on reality.

"I grew up knowing the fame is transient," she wisely observed. "At the moment, my fame eclipses my dad's.

It's my little time to shine. That's a bittersweet thing, which my dad has handled gracefully.'' But she also knew that like her dad, she wouldn't stay on top forever.

Maybe this was the reason that success and fame hadn't changed her priorities either. When she could have simply rested in a fancy hotel, she would still play a gig in Waco, Texas, and race the ninety miles back to Dallas to catch a plane in the middle of the night, just so that she could fly back to Nashville and spend time with her son on a fishing trip. It might have been because of the experiences of her youth, but she still knew what was really important. And she also knew that her most challenging job was not as a singer, songwriter, performer, or producer, it was as a mother.

''It is a difficult thing to be a working mom,'' Pam flatly admitted. That is something that many show business women have said, but they said it simply about their business. Just like she had long done through her music, Tillis expressed her concerns as if they were the concerns of every working woman. And they were. Even in parenting, Pam had her finger on what other women went through every day. One of the reasons she continued to win more and more female fans is that Pam never seemed to put her problems ahead of everyone else's. She really believed that while she did something unique for living, she really was just like everyone else. The more the fans saw this, the more they loved her!

''I really admire Vince Gill for using his success in such a positive way,'' she told *Country Music*. ''I think everybody wants to do [the same] . . . to me, a real motivating force is to do something that's timeless, to write a classic like a 'Green Green Grass of Home' or record an album like Willie Nelson's 'Stardust,' just something that lasts forever.'' And that is probably the thinking that kept her racing home to be a mom even when it would have been a lot easier to make a telephone call and go to sleep. Pam Tillis recognized that relationships were something that lasted forever, and she worked at them even harder than she did finding songs.

The woman who calls herself the "anxiety-ridden perfectionist" who is constantly searching for her "masterpiece," has come a long way since being born in Plant City, Florida, the product of a teenage girl's romance with a struggling entertainer. She has survived brutal injuries in a car wreck, a less-than-perfect childhood, a bad marriage, and a few dozen bad breaks. And these situations, which have broken so many others, simply make this determined lady even stronger. She became a builder. And what she has built is more than a career. While escaping from a large shadow and becoming a star, she has also found love and self-esteem. Like few others, Pam Tillis is a success both on and off the stage. And not unlike Cleopatra, there is no denying that this woman is something special who has changed the world in a way that few thought possible. She has gone where no woman has gone before, and she is just beginning!